C000276838

The Silent Guru

Wasyl Nimenko

Goalpath Books

The Silent Guru

978-1-908142-59-7

Published in Great Britain 2020

Copyright © Wasyl Nimenko 2020

Goalpath Books

The right of Wasyl Nimenko to be identified as the author of this work has been asserted in accordance with the Copyright, Designs and Patents Act 1988.

All rights reserved. No part of this publication may be reproduced, stored in a retrieval system, or transmitted in any form or by any means electronic, mechanical, photocopying, recording or otherwise, without the prior permission of the publishers.

Wasyl Nimenko was born in Ipswich, England. His mother was a staunch Catholic from the O'Dowd clan in the west of Ireland and his father was a staunch Atheist from Dnipropetrovsk in eastern Ukraine.

Wasyl studied medicine in London then psychotherapy with Anthony Storr and Ian Gordon-Brown. From 1982-1991 he worked with survivors of torture. He has worked independently, in the NHS and with the homeless.

Although Wasyl brings his experience from working in medicine and transpersonal psychology, the path he took is based on eastern spiritual disciplines and so the theme of his writing focuses on inner happiness.

ALSO BY WASYL NIMENKO

The Fool's Poems
The Fool's Poems II
The Cave
Face to Face With Death
Carl Jung and Ramana Maharshi
The Spiritual Nature of Addictions
Research and Papers
Notes From the Inside
Understanding Stillness
Stillness
Solitude
Searching in Secret Solitude
Invisible Bullets
Searching in Secret Orkney
Searching in Secret Ukraine
Searching in Secret New Zealand and Australia
Searching in Secret India

The Sage

Like Groundhog Day, it can seem that repeated effort keeps on returning us to the same place. But with perseverance, eventually we see who we are and we are released.

The boy was tired. It had been a long afternoon of walking. As he approached a crossroads he could see there were no signs. He was looking for somewhere to stay the night to break his journey south.

A group of three men were talking just a few yards down the right hand turning. They stopped talking as he approached. He felt much younger than them but decided to ask them if there was somewhere to stay the night.

'Are there rooms or a hostel to stay nearby?

'Nothing around here.' Said the broadest man.

'How far until there is one?'

'Half a day's journey straight on to the next village.' Said the tallest of the three men.

'So there is nothing else?'

'No.' said the tall man again. The other men nodded in agreement. 'Not unless you want to stay the night with the beggars in an old graveyard."

'No.' The boy said. But to his surprise he kept looking at the tall man, as if the man hadn't finished and had something else to say.

'Nothing other than that.' The tall man said. 'You will have to walk fast to get to the next village before the light goes.'

'How far is the graveyard?'

'An hour and a half.' Turn left just here and it's towards the hills. The road ends and there's nothing. It's arid land. But if you keep walking straight, eventually you'll see some old gravestones. No one goes there.

1

They say only beggars live there.'

Two hours later the boy came to the end of the road. There was just a gentle rise in the ground towards the hills over the next half a mile. He stopped and looked around. Here there was nothing except the occasional slightly raised areas of ground. He thought these must be the old graves the men mentioned.

The area looked as if it was not tended by any relatives of the people buried there. There were some low laying shrubs between some of the trees which were about every thirty yards apart. He guessed that there couldn't be more than about thirty to forty people buried here in this graveyard.

Apart from the graves, the only evidence that man had marked this area was a small building he could see in the distance at the far end of the graveyard. Now that he had arrived, the boy was more interested in sitting under the shade of a tree to rest his body from the walking. He put his bag against a tree, sat resting his back against it and fell into a deep sleep.

The boy woke in the darkness looking up at the stars which now surrounded him. He could see there was a light in the distance and it was coming towards him. As the light got closer to him he could see it was a lamp being carried by a man.

He sat motionless in case the man with the light hadn't noticed him and would walk on. Was it the beggar the men had mentioned? Slowly and quite definitely someone was moving towards him.

He wondered if the beggar had spotted him or if this was just the usual path they used. The boy sat still and waited. But he felt uncomfortable sitting so he stood up waiting for the light to approach him closer. Eventually it stopped several yards from him.

From behind the light of the oil lamp the man's hand beckoned him to follow.

'I was travelling south. I was too tired to carry on so I was looking for a hostel to stay a night. I was told this was the nearest place I might be able to stay. Is it ok to stay?' said the boy.

The old man didn't speak.

The boy followed the man back to where the light had first appeared in the direction of the building he had noticed before he had fallen asleep.

When they entered the building, the boy noticed there was no other light apart from the light from the oil lamp which the old man held and which he now placed on the floor. Against the wall were some hessian cushions. The boy noticed a table but otherwise the room seemed empty.

The old man handed the boy a bowl of soup and a cup of water and pointed to the hessian cushions and the boy knew this was his bed. It was home for the night.

The boy felt he had arrived somewhere very strange and also that the man was strange. He had not even spoken. Then he realised the man had communicated everything perfectly in silence.

＊

The boy woke to rays of early morning sunlight reflected off the white painted walls and the shiny stone floor of the room which now seemed simple, clean and comfortable. He sat up to see the old man facing a window. The old man was sitting still with his eyes closed facing the hills through the window. The boy watched him and became aware that the man seemed to radiate a peacefulness which brought the boys mind to a state of being very conscious of his thoughts. It was as if the old man was showing him something and he was inviting him to follow his example.

After some time sitting still looking at the old man the boy noticed the old man open his eyes. He looked straight ahead out of the window at the hills. After some more time he spoke.

'Why you are here?'

'As I said last night, I was just looking for a place to stay the night. I am on my way south. It seems very peaceful here.'

'There is no more peaceful place than inside your self.'

The man was still for some time. Then he asked the boy, 'Who are you?'

'I am from up north of the river. I am travelling south looking for a better life. My family are unhappy and make me unhappy. The world of business they are connected to doesn't interest me at all. I am looking for something deeper, with meaning. For true happiness.'

'These are the two questions which you should ask every day at the beginning of your day.' There was a

4

pause almost as if he wanted the boy to remember.

'The answer to Why am I here is this. It is to find the happiness which is inside you.' He paused again, once more so as if that the boy could remember what he had said.

'The answer to the Who am I is this. You find out by finding out what you are not. You say you are not this and not that. You are not your thoughts. You are not a collection of thoughts which is called the ego.' He paused again as if to let the boy absorb what he had said.

'What is really you is not your body. It is not your memories or your thoughts about the future. You are simply consciousness without thoughts.' He paused again.

'What has always been there aware of all your thoughts is your consciousness. It is what sees without eyes, what hears without ears. That is what you are.' There was one last pause, the longest.

'Seeing that you are this consciousness of everything, which is the same as the consciousness of the universe, you eventually see this is in truth what you are. So you must actually be it.

'Every morning when you sit in stillness ask, Why am I here? The answer is to be happy inside. Then ask, Who am I? The answer is realised by seeing what you are not. I am not this, not that. I am consciousness. I am that I am, which is everything. I am that.'

'How do you know this?' The boy asked.

'It is what I studied and practiced my whole life. It is the art of being happy by looking within for happiness.'

'You are here as an old man, alone. Does it work?'

'Yes. But that is enough. If you want to know more I will have to tell you tomorrow. I must go and get some food.'

The old man got up and took a hessian bag with him as he walked out of the door towards the direction of the road.

When the old man had gone the boy took out a pencil and a notebook and wrote down what the man had told him.

✳

The next morning the boy was once again woken by the rays of sunlight reflecting off the walls and the shiny floor.

The old man was sitting still with his eyes closed facing the hills through the window. The boy watched him and became aware that the man seemed to radiate a peacefulness which brought the boys mind to a state of being very conscious of his thoughts. It was as if the old man was showing him something and he was inviting him to follow his example.

When the old man opened his eyes from looking out the window, as he had done the day before, he turned to the boy and spoke again.

'Every morning when you sit in stillness ask, Why am I here? The answer is to be happy inside. Then ask, Who am I? The answer is realised by seeing what you are not. I am not this, not that. I am consciousness. I am that I am, which is everything. I am that.'

6

∞

'The ancient civilisations knew it. They knew that happiness was inside. In Judaism, when Moses asked God for his name he answered, "I Am That I Am. Thus shalt you say unto the children of Israel, I Am has sent me to you." Jehovah means I am. So knowing the self, God is known as they are taken to be the same.' He paused.

∞

'The Pashupati Seal is a soapstone seal discovered at the Mohenjo-daro archaeological site of the Indus Valley Civilisation. It is estimated to have been carved around 2350 BC and is thought to be the earliest prototype of the God Shiva. The seal shows a seated cross-legged figure in the yogic 'padmasama' or lotus meditation posture with arms pointing downwards. It is important because it is one of the first communications from our ancient ancestors which reflects the stillness of silently looking inwards.'

∞

'In Hinduism the mind is helped to look inwards by "Netti Netti," from the Brihadaranyaka Upanishad written around 800 BC, meaning, "Neither this neither that," which helps the mind to constantly disidentify with anything other than that which is everything.'

∞

'One of the ancient Greek's key instructions, "Know the self." was written on the portals of their most important temple, the Temple of Apollo in Delphi.'

∞

'In the Hebrew Bible or the Tanaka, in Psalm 46, God is assumed to be inside, "Be still and know that I am God."

∞

'And again in Christianity in Luke 17, it says, "The kingdom of God is within you." Do you see it?'

∞

'Even Shakespeare pointed man strongly inside,' "This above all-to thine own self be true."

∞

'So you see, they all say that happiness is inside. We have to be that consciousness not just in the morning when we sit still. But gradually we become that consciousness 'I Am' more and more throughout the day. We surrender to it. We surrender our Self to the Universe. Then we become it.'

'How do you know this?' The boy asked.

'It is what I studied and practiced my whole life. It is the art of being happy by looking within for happiness.'

'If you want to know more I will have to tell you tomorrow. I must go and get some food.'

The old man got up and took a hessian bag with him as he walked out of the door towards the direction of the road.

When the old man had gone the boy took out a pencil and a notebook and wrote down what the man had told him.

*

The next morning the boy was once again woken by the rays of sunlight reflecting off the walls and the shiny floor.

The old man was sitting still with his eyes closed facing the hills through the window. The boy watched him and became aware that the man seemed to radiate a peacefulness which brought the boys mind to a state of being very conscious of his thoughts. It was as if the old man was showing him something and he was inviting him to follow his example.

When the old man opened his eyes from looking out the window, as he had done the day before, he turned to the boy and spoke again.

'Every morning when you sit in stillness ask, Why am I here? The answer is to be happy inside. Then ask, Who am I? The answer is realised by seeing what you are not. I am not this, not that. I am consciousness. I am that I am, which is everything. I am that.'

∞

'Happiness can't be acquired like a possession. You may have looked at acquiring money, things, power, influence or knowledge to make you happy. You may have looked at having all of these possessions to make you happy. But these will make you bored and you will endlessly keep going onto the next best thing. Possessions lead to fear of their use and loss. Fear and loss make us think we will be happier if we can more securely possess them, so an endless pursuit begins. Loss anxiety makes us try harder to possess what does not even make us happy.'

∞

'Don't be misled by beauty because Beauty is something recognised outside, happiness is always inside. Beauty is derived from the senses, happiness is revealed inside. Beauty is a synthesis of fine thinking, happiness is simply being in the heart with no thoughts.'

∞

'There is no relationship between any form of possession and happiness.'

∞

'How do we know this? A powerful wealthy influential person will always have loss anxiety about their securities. They cannot be as happy as the person who has found happiness inside. Seeing that acquiring things, money, power, influence or knowledge does not make you happy, there is only one place left to look for happiness. Inside.'

'How do you know this?' The boy asked.

'It is what I studied and practiced my whole life. It is the art of being happy by looking within for happiness.'

'You are here as an old man, alone. Does it work?'

'Yes. But that is enough. If you want to know more I will have to tell you tomorrow. I must go and get some food.'

The old man got up and took a hessian bag with him as he walked out of the door towards the direction of the road.

When the old man had gone the boy took out a pencil and a notebook and wrote down what the man had told him.

*

The next morning the boy was once again woken by the rays of sunlight reflecting off the walls and the shiny floor.

The old man was sitting still with his eyes closed facing the hills through the window. The boy watched him and became aware that the man seemed to radiate a peacefulness which brought the boys mind to a state of being very conscious of his thoughts. It was as if the old man was showing him something and he was inviting him to follow his example.

When the old man opened his eyes from looking out

the window, as he had done the day before, he turned to the boy and spoke again.

'Every morning when you sit in stillness ask, Why am I here? The answer is to be happy inside. Then ask, Who am I? The answer is realised by seeing what you are not. I am not this, not that. I am consciousness. I am that I am, which is everything. I am that.'

∞

'To be happy you need to see you can't acquire it by adding something to yourself. Instead, see that you have to remove something about you. Get rid of your belief that you can acquire happiness by seeing you already have it.'

∞

'Happiness is seen by getting rid of looking outside of you for happiness.'

∞

'Happiness is seen by getting rid of thinking security of any kind will make you happy.'

∞

'Happiness is seen by getting rid of searching for happiness because it is already inside you.'

∞

'Happiness is seen by constant effort to be happy.'

∞

'Happiness is experienced by seeing happiness is not hidden but that you have just been looking outside for happiness when all along it is inside.'

'How do you know this?' The boy asked.

'It is what I studied and practiced my whole life. It is the art of being happy by looking within for happiness.'

'You are here as an old man, alone. Does it work?'

'Yes. But that is enough. If you want to know more I will have to tell you tomorrow. I must go and get some food.'

The old man got up and took a hessian bag with him as he walked out of the door towards the direction of the road.

When the old man had gone the boy took out a pencil and a notebook and wrote down what the man had told him.

✱

The next morning the boy was once again woken by the rays of sunlight reflecting off the walls and the shiny floor.

The old man was sitting still with his eyes closed facing the hills through the window. The boy watched him and became aware that the man seemed to radiate a peacefulness which brought the boys mind to a state of being very conscious of his thoughts. It was as if the old man was showing him something and he was inviting him to follow his example.

When the old man opened his eyes from looking out the window, as he had done the day before, he turned to the boy and spoke again.

'Every morning when you sit in stillness ask, Why am I here? The answer is to be happy inside. Then ask, Who am I? The answer is realised by seeing what you are not. I am not this, not that. I am consciousness. I am that I am, which is everything. I am that.'

∞

'You can only ever be happy today, only in the present, only today, only right now.'

∞

'You can only be happy today, in the present, right now, so give up the search in the future, so you can see it now.'

∞

'Happiness is inside and we can only be happy right now today.

∞

'To access happiness we have to get rid of thinking it is outside or in the future.'

∞

'Like light is always here from the sun but we may be busy looking at something else; we only need to turn inside to see our happiness.'

∞

'We may not be able to be happy all the time but our happiness is always here inside us.'

∞

'Your happiness depends on seeing your happiness is already inside you and is not something new which can be acquired from outside.'

'How do you know this?' The boy asked.

'It is what I studied and practiced my whole life. It is the art of being happy by looking within for happiness.'

'You are here as an old man, alone. Does it work?'

'Yes. But that is enough. If you want to know more I will have to tell you tomorrow. I must go and get some food.'

The old man got up and took a hessian bag with him as he walked out of the door towards the direction of the road.

When the old man had gone the boy took out a pencil and a notebook and wrote down what the man had told him.

*

The next morning the boy was once again woken by the rays of sunlight reflecting off the walls and the shiny floor.

The old man was sitting still with his eyes closed facing the hills through the window. The boy watched him and became aware that the man seemed to radiate a peacefulness which brought the boys mind to a state of being very conscious of his thoughts. It was as if the old man was showing him something and he was inviting him to follow his example.

When the old man opened his eyes from looking out the window, as he had done the day before, he turned to the boy and spoke again.

'Every morning when you sit in stillness ask, Why am I here? The answer is to be happy inside. Then ask, Who am I? The answer is realised by seeing what you are not. I am not this, not that. I am consciousness. I am that I am, which is everything. I am that.'

∞

'To be happy now, you have to be happy with what you are, with what you have.'

∞

'To be happy with what you are and what you have is

to be happy with just sufficient.'

∞

'Sufficient is what is enough. Enough for how long? Well today is how long.'

'How do you know this?' The boy asked.

'It is what I studied and practiced my whole life. It is the art of being happy by looking within for happiness.'

'You are here as an old man, alone. Does it work?'

'Yes. But that is enough. If you want to know more I will have to tell you tomorrow. I must go and get some food.'

The old man got up and took a hessian bag with him as he walked out of the door towards the direction of the road.

When the old man had gone the boy took out a pencil and a notebook and wrote down what the man had told him.

✽

The next morning the boy was once again woken by the rays of sunlight reflecting off the walls and the shiny floor.

The old man was sitting still with his eyes closed facing the hills through the window. The boy watched him and became aware that the man seemed to radiate a peacefulness which brought the boys mind to a state of being very conscious of his thoughts. It was as if the old man was showing him something and he was inviting

17

him to follow his example.

When the old man opened his eyes from looking out the window, as he had done the day before, he turned to the boy and spoke again.

'Every morning when you sit in stillness ask, Why am I here? The answer is to be happy inside. Then ask, Who am I? The answer is realised by seeing what you are not. I am not this, not that. I am consciousness. I am that I am, which is everything. I am that.'

∞

'When you see you are as happy as you can be today without wanting anything, you have found happiness. When you see this you see you have no want. When you see you have no want you cannot be happier. Do you know a person with no want?'

∞

'The easiest way to make yourself an exile from your happiness is to start thinking about ~~what you want~~ in the future.'

what you 'Must' have

∞

'There are only three things we don't see about happiness. The first is that to access happiness we have to get rid of thinking it is outside. Like light is always here from the sun but we may be busy looking at something else; we only need to turn inside to see our happiness. We may not be able to be happy all the time but our happiness is always here inside us. Your happiness depends on seeing your happiness is already inside you and is not something new which can be acquired from outside.'

∞

'The second is that you can't actually ever be happy tomorrow, only today. You can only be happy today, in the present, right now, so give up the search in the future, so you can see it now. Happiness is inside and we can only be happy right now today.'

∞

'The third is that to be happy now, you have to be happy with what you have and have no want. To be happy with what you are and what you have is to be happy with just sufficient. Sufficient is what is enough. Enough for how long? Well today is how long.'
'How do you know this?' The boy asked.
'It is what I studied and practiced my whole life. It is the art of being happy by looking within for happiness.'
'You are here as an old man, alone. Does it work?'
'Yes. But that is enough. If you want to know more I will have to tell you tomorrow. I must go and get some food.'
The old man got up and took a hessian bag with him as he walked out of the door towards the direction of the road.
When the old man had gone the boy took out a pencil

and a notebook and wrote down what the man had told him.

*

The next morning the boy was once again woken by the rays of sunlight reflecting off the walls and the shiny floor.

The old man was sitting still with his eyes closed facing the hills through the window. The boy watched him and became aware that the man seemed to radiate a peacefulness which brought the boys mind to a state of being very conscious of his thoughts. It was as if the old man was showing him something and he was inviting him to follow his example.

When the old man opened his eyes from looking out the window, as he had done the day before, he turned to the boy and spoke again.

'Every morning when you sit in stillness ask, Why am I here? The answer is to be happy inside. Then ask, Who am I? The answer is realised by seeing what you are not. I am not this, not that. I am consciousness. I am that I am, which is everything. I am that.'

∞

'Seeing our goal is inner stillness, we try to use thinking to find it but we can only find our stillness by being still, not by thinking about it.'

∞

'When we look inside at 'Who are we?' we become conscious we are not thought.'

'It is a surprise to discover that you are not your thoughts, which through meditation seem like imposters.'

∞

'We are taught and programmed to believe we are a bundle of thoughts called the ego.'

∞

'But in meditation you see you are not just a bundle of thoughts.'

∞

'When you stay with this you begin to see consciousness comes before thought. Consciousness is always here. Thought comes and goes.'

∞

'In meditation you see you are consciousness which is not a thought but is what creates thought.'

∞

'There is no more mystery.'

21

∞

'There is no more misery about our thinking.'

∞

'In wanting to see what we are, it is essential to ask and find out what we are not.'

∞

'We think we are our memories, but these are just thoughts, so if we believe this, we can easily take ourselves to be what we are not. We may think we are what we imagine in the future but this is just thought and is not what we are now.'

∞

'In asking what you are and what you are not, you see you are not your thoughts but consciousness, which is responsible for thoughts.'

∞

'When something is made up it has no authenticity; just as you always know when an actor is acting.'

∞

'The same mistaken authenticity is obvious when

our ignorance of believing we are the ego is uncovered.'

∞

'You can see what you are is consciousness of stillness inside you.'

∞

'Consciousness of inner stillness lets us see our inner self is stillness.'

∞

'Consciousness of inner stillness lets us see that our inner self is our natural happiness.'

∞

'Our answer to what we are is I am just 'I am,' the consciousness we all have of inner stillness.'

'How do you know this?' The boy asked.

'It is what I studied and practiced my whole life. It is the art of being happy by looking within for happiness.'

'You are here as an old man, alone. Does it work?'

'Yes. But that is enough. If you want to know more I will have to tell you tomorrow. I must go and get some food.'

The old man got up and took a hessian bag with him as he walked out of the door towards the direction of the road.

When the old man had gone the boy took out a pencil and a notebook and wrote down what the man had told him.

*

The next morning the boy was once again woken by the rays of sunlight reflecting off the walls and the shiny floor.

The old man was sitting still with his eyes closed facing the hills through the window. The boy watched him and became aware that the man seemed to radiate a peacefulness which brought the boys mind to a state of being very conscious of his thoughts. It was as if the old man was showing him something and he was inviting him to follow his example.

When the old man opened his eyes from looking out the window, as he had done the day before, he turned to the boy and spoke again.

'Every morning when you sit in stillness ask, Why am I here? The answer is to be happy inside. Then ask, Who am I? The answer is realised by seeing what you are not. I am not this, not that. I am consciousness. I am that I am, which is everything. I am that.'

∞

'When we see what the world is like and that what we do doesn't work, we realise that to be our inner self, we have to surrender to what we trust.'

'What we trust is either inside us or outside us.'

∞

'The first path may be to look inside and enquire into what is our nature and to surrender to that.'

∞

'The other path is to look to something outside us. It can be a place of pilgrimage, a mountain, a god or a saint. Then surrender to that.'

∞

'Whichever path we take, we eventually see we have surrendered to our inner self.'

∞

'When we see this we can keep or withdraw the projection but it makes no difference as all is seen as one.'

'How do you know this?' The boy asked.

'It is what I studied and practiced my whole life. It is the art of being happy by looking within for happiness.'

'You are here as an old man, alone. Does it work?'

'Yes. But that is enough. If you want to know more I will have to tell you tomorrow. I must go and get some food.'

The old man got up and took a hessian bag with him as he walked out of the door towards the direction of the road.

When the old man had gone the boy took out a pencil and a notebook and wrote down what the man had told him.

*

The next morning the boy was once again woken by the rays of sunlight reflecting off the walls and the shiny floor.

The old man was sitting still with his eyes closed facing the hills through the window. The boy watched him and became aware that the man seemed to radiate a peacefulness which brought the boys mind to a state of being very conscious of his thoughts. It was as if the old man was showing him something and he was inviting him to follow his example.

When the old man opened his eyes from looking out the window, as he had done the day before, he turned to the boy and spoke again.

'Every morning when you sit in stillness ask, Why am I here? The answer is to be happy inside. Then ask, Who am I? The answer is realised by seeing what you are not. I am not this, not that. I am consciousness. I am that I am, which is everything. I am that.'

∞

'We are not born unhappy but our circumstances make us unhappy, so we try to find the happiness we know is inside. This is our nature.'

∞

'Our happiness is our self which is the same as everything in the Universe and no different from it.'

∞

'Religions point to seeing our inner self as our higher power inside as God. Most simply this is consciousness of "I am." This can be seen in the words from the east and the west over the last three thousand years. Let me remind you of what I said the ancients knew before I bring you to the modern age.'

∞

'When Moses asked God for his name he answered,' "I Am That I Am. Thus shalt you say unto the children of Israel, I Am has sent me to you." 'Jehovah means I am. So knowing the self, God is known as they are taken to be the same.'

∞

"Netti Netti' means, "Neither this neither this," 'Which helps the mind to constantly disidentify with anything other than that which is everything.

∞

"Know the self." 'Comes from the Temple of Apollo, in Delphi in Greece.'

∞

"Be still and know that I am God," 'Is from Psalm 46.' "The kingdom of God is within you," 'Is from Luke.'

∞

'Over a thousand years ago an Indian Guru called Shankara wrote in a series of verses called Vivekachudamani,' "Even after the Truth has been realised, there remains that strong, obstinate impression that one is still an ego - the agent and experiencer. This has to be carefully removed by living in a state of constant identification with the supreme non-dual Self. Full Awakening is the eventual ceasing of all the mental impressions of being an ego."

∞

"This above all-to thine own self be true," 'Was written by Shakespeare.'

∞

'All of this was most clearly summarised by another Indian Guru, Ramana Maharshi when he said in 1937, "Your duty is to be and not to be this or that. 'I AM that I AM' sums up the whole truth. The method is summarised in 'Be still.' What does 'stillness' mean? It means 'destroy yourself.' Because any form or shape is the cause of trouble. Give up the notion that, I am so and so."

∞

'Again going back to Shankara, he also said this about the ego and the self. "The fool takes the reflection of the sun in the water of a pot to be the sun; the wise man eliminates pot, water, and reflection and knows the sun in the sky as it really is, single and unaffected, but illuminating all three. In the same way the fool through error and misperception, identifies himself with the ego and its reflected light experienced through the medium of the intellect. The wise and discriminating man eliminates body, intellect, and reflected light of consciousness and probes deeply into his real Self which illuminates all three while remaining uniform in the ether of the heart. Thereby he realises the eternal witness which is absolute knowledge, illuminating all three."

'How do you know this?' The boy asked.

'It is what I studied and practiced my whole life. It is the art of being happy by looking within for happiness.'

'You are here as an old man, alone. Does it work?'

'Yes. But that is enough. If you want to know more I will have to tell you tomorrow. I must go and get some food.'

The old man got up and took a hessian bag with him as he walked out of the door towards the direction of the road.

When the old man had gone the boy took out a pencil and a notebook and wrote down what the man had told him.

*

The next morning the boy was once again woken by the rays of sunlight reflecting off the walls and the shiny floor.

The old man was sitting still with his eyes closed facing the hills through the window. The boy watched him and became aware that the man seemed to radiate a peacefulness which brought the boys mind to a state of being very conscious of his thoughts. It was as if the old man was showing him something and he was inviting him to follow his example.

When the old man opened his eyes from looking out the window, as he had done the day before, he turned to the boy and spoke again.

'Every morning when you sit in stillness ask, Why am I here? The answer is to be happy inside. Then ask, Who am I? The answer is realised by seeing what you are not. I am not this, not that. I am consciousness. I am that I am, which is everything. I am that.'

∞

'Meditation is turning inwards to find inner

happiness.'

∞

'When we see what we are our searching ends.'

∞

'Somehow we discover that between our thoughts, is our inner stillness.'

∞

'Whatever way we reach this stillness and surrender to it, is our own meditation, our own truth.'

∞

'How do you know this?' The boy asked.

'It is what I studied and practiced my whole life. It is the art of being happy by looking within for happiness.'

'You are here as an old man, alone. Does it work?'

'Yes. But that is enough. If you want to know more I will have to tell you tomorrow. I must go and get some food.'

The old man got up and took a hessian bag with him as he walked out of the door towards the direction of the road.

When the old man had gone the boy took out a pencil and a notebook and wrote down what the man had told him.

*

The next morning the boy was once again woken by the rays of sunlight reflecting off the walls and the shiny floor.

The old man was sitting still with his eyes closed facing the hills through the window. The boy watched him and became aware that the man seemed to radiate a peacefulness which brought the boys mind to a state of being very conscious of his thoughts. It was as if the old man was showing him something and he was inviting him to follow his example.

When the old man opened his eyes from looking out the window, as he had done the day before, he turned to the boy and spoke again.

'Every morning when you sit in stillness ask, Why am I here? The answer is to be happy inside. Then ask, Who am I? The answer is realised by seeing what you are not. I am not this, not that. I am consciousness. I am that I am, which is everything. I am that.'

∞

'There is not one way to meditate. But there is only one final pathway.'

∞

'There are no techniques to meditate. But there are different levels of attainment in meditation.'

∞

'What we desire to be happy is to stop thoughts, to let us experience our stillness.'

∞

'To meditate we need to withdraw inside to experience this one thing only.'

∞

'There are different levels of attainment in meditation we may be able to experience.'

∞

'Our level of attainment may be different at different times for each of us.'

∞

'If we find it difficult to start by withdrawing inside to see what we are and what we are not, we can turn inwards and gain some control of our mind by tethering it to one thing by following our breathing.'

∞

'Next, we can turn inwards, tethering our mind by

repeating a silent sound a mantra.'

∞

'Meditation shows us we seem conditioned to keep on having thoughts instead of just being still without thoughts.'

∞

'Meditation is repeatedly stopping thoughts to let us be this inner stillness. The battle resumes every time we meditate.'

∞

'The more we meditate, the more we see thoughts are not us and so the battle of our consciousness against them becomes more effective. '

∞

'To be conscious of what we are as stillness is all we need to do. This consciousness of 'I am' is all we can be

∞

'We do not add anything to us to meditate. It is removal. We remove what is not us . . . thought. The reward is the indescribable conscious happiness of stillness.'

34

∞

'The method, path and goal of meditation are contained in the Biblical statement,' "Be still and know that I am God."

∞

'In other words, searching and seeing inner stillness with no thought is the method. Being conscious of 'I Am' is the only truth.'

'How do you know this?' The boy asked.

'It is what I studied and practiced my whole life. It is the art of being happy by looking within for happiness.'

'You are here as an old man, alone. Does it work?'

'Yes. But that is enough. If you want to know more I will have to tell you tomorrow. I must go and get some food.'

The old man got up and took a hessian bag with him as he walked out of the door towards the direction of the road.

When the old man had gone the boy took out a pencil and a notebook and wrote down what the man had told him.

*

The next morning the boy was once again woken by the rays of sunlight reflecting off the walls and the shiny floor.

The old man was sitting still with his eyes closed facing the hills through the window. The boy watched him and became aware that the man seemed to radiate a peacefulness which brought the boys mind to a state of being very conscious of his thoughts. It was as if the old man was showing him something and he was inviting him to follow his example.

When the old man opened his eyes from looking out the window, as he had done the day before, he turned to the boy and spoke again.

'Every morning when you sit in stillness ask, Why am I here? The answer is to be happy inside.'

'Then ask, Who am I? The answer is realised by seeing what you are not. I am not this, not that. I am consciousness. I am that I am, which is everything. I am that.'

∞

'Religions know we prefer mystery to reality.'

∞

'Maybe religion keeps you hoping there is a better place. Spirituality shows you that you are already here.'

'How do you know this?' The boy asked.

'It is what I studied and practiced my whole life. It is the art of being happy by looking within for happiness.'

'You are here as an old man, alone. Does it work?'

'Yes. But that is enough. If you want to know more I will have to tell you tomorrow. I must go and get some food.'

The old man got up and took a hessian bag with him as he walked out of the door towards the direction of the road.

When the old man had gone the boy took out a pencil and a notebook and wrote down what the man had told him.

*

The next morning the boy was once again woken by the rays of sunlight reflecting off the walls and the shiny floor.

The old man was sitting still with his eyes closed facing the hills through the window. The boy watched him and became aware that the man seemed to radiate a peacefulness which brought the boys mind to a state of being very conscious of his thoughts. It was as if the old man was showing him something and he was inviting him to follow his example.

When the old man opened his eyes from looking out the window, as he had done the day before, he turned to the boy and spoke again.

'Every morning when you sit in stillness ask, Why am I here? The answer is to be happy inside. Then ask, Who am I? The answer is realised by seeing what you are not. I am not this, not that. I am consciousness. I am that I am, which is everything. I am that.'

∞

'Receiving kindness, even if it is just being listened to, can restore our belief in mankind, that there are decent people.'

∞

'Even though kindness is intangible it is our most precious treasure because it can give us a purpose in life, which we can pass on.'

∞

'When kindness is not present it is time for extensive looking. Why has all the pain hit so hard that it stops kindness to our self and others?'

'How do you know this?' The boy asked.

'It is what I studied and practiced my whole life. It is the art of being happy by looking within for happiness.'

'You are here as an old man, alone. Does it work?'

'Yes. But that is enough. If you want to know more I will have to tell you tomorrow. I must go and get some food.'

The old man got up and took a hessian bag with him as he walked out of the door towards the direction of the road.

When the old man had gone the boy took out a pencil and a notebook and wrote down what the man had told him.

✻

The next morning the boy was once again woken by the rays of sunlight reflecting off the walls and the shiny floor.

The old man was sitting still with his eyes closed facing the hills through the window. The boy watched him and became aware that the man seemed to radiate a peacefulness which brought the boys mind to a state of being very conscious of his thoughts. It was as if the old man was showing him something and he was inviting him to follow his example.

When the old man opened his eyes from looking out the window, as he had done the day before, he turned to the boy and spoke again.

'Every morning when you sit in stillness ask, Why am I here? The answer is to be happy inside. Then ask, Who am I? The answer is realised by seeing what you are not. I am not this, not that. I am consciousness. I am that I am, which is everything. I am that.'

∞

'Without humility there can be no learning.'

'How do you know this?' The boy asked.

'It is what I studied and practiced my whole life. It is the art of being happy by looking within for happiness.'

'You are here as an old man, alone. Does it work?'

'Yes. But that is enough. If you want to know more I will have to tell you tomorrow. I must go and get some food.'

The old man got up and took a hessian bag with him as he walked out of the door towards the direction of the road.

When the old man had gone the boy took out a pencil and a notebook and wrote down what the man had told him.

✳

The next morning the boy was once again woken by the rays of sunlight reflecting off the walls and the shiny floor.

The old man was sitting still with his eyes closed facing the hills through the window. The boy watched him and became aware that the man seemed to radiate a peacefulness which brought the boy's mind to a state of being very conscious of his thoughts. It was as if the old man was showing him something and he was inviting him to follow his example.

When the old man opened his eyes from looking out the window, as he had done the day before, he turned to the boy and spoke again.

'Every morning when you sit in stillness ask, Why am I here? The answer is to be happy inside. Then ask, Who am I? The answer is realised by seeing what you are not. I am not this, not that. I am consciousness. I am that I am, which is everything. I am that.'

∞

'We become so involved with thoughts; we actually see them as being us, instead of seeing them only like passing clouds in the sky.'

∞

'Detachment is separating our processes from other people's processes whilst still having a relationship.'

'How do you know this?' The boy asked.

'It is what I studied and practiced my whole life. It is the art of being happy by looking within for happiness.'

'You are here as an old man, alone. Does it work?'

'Yes. But that is enough. If you want to know more I will have to tell you tomorrow. I must go and get some food.'

The old man got up and took a hessian bag with him as he walked out of the door towards the direction of the road.

When the old man had gone the boy took out a pencil and a notebook and wrote down what the man had told him.

*

The next morning the boy was once again woken by the rays of sunlight reflecting off the walls and the shiny floor.

The old man was sitting still with his eyes closed facing the hills through the window. The boy watched him and became aware that the man seemed to radiate a peacefulness which brought the boys mind to a state of being very conscious of his thoughts. It was as if the old man was showing him something and he was inviting him to follow his example.

When the old man opened his eyes from looking out the window, as he had done the day before, he turned to the boy and spoke again.

'Every morning when you sit in stillness ask, Why am I here? The answer is to be happy inside. Then ask, Who am I? The answer is realised by seeing what you are not. I am not this, not that. I am consciousness. I am that I am, which is everything. I am that.'

∞

'Solitude is an attitude detaching us from the distractions of the world.'

∞

'Solitude lets us detach from the distractions of the world, to experience happiness inside.'

∞

'Seeing our happiness is inside, we begin to spend more time in solitude and also with those whose view of the world is like ours.'

∞

'Being our self is none other than being conscious of the happiness of stillness inside.'

'How do you know this?' The boy asked.

'It is what I studied and practiced my whole life. It is

the art of being happy by looking within for happiness.'

'You are here as an old man, alone. Does it work?'

'Yes. But that is enough. If you want to know more I will have to tell you tomorrow. I must go and get some food.'

The old man got up and took a hessian bag with him as he walked out of the door towards the direction of the road.

When the old man had gone the boy took out a pencil and a notebook and wrote down what the man had told him.

*

The next morning the boy was once again woken by the rays of sunlight reflecting off the walls and the shiny floor.

The old man was sitting still with his eyes closed facing the hills through the window. The boy watched him and became aware that the man seemed to radiate a peacefulness which brought the boys mind to a state of being very conscious of his thoughts. It was as if the old man was showing him something and he was inviting him to follow his example.

When the old man opened his eyes from looking out the window, as he had done the day before, he turned to the boy and spoke again.

'Every morning when you sit in stillness ask, Why am I here? The answer is to be happy inside. Then ask, Who am I? The answer is realised by seeing what you are not. I am not this, not that. I am consciousness. I am that

I am, which is everything. I am that.'

∞

'Silence is the language of stillness.

∞

'Consciousness of inner stillness, happiness and truth are perhaps only words for the same thing.'

∞

'There are no words for consciousness of stillness.'
'How do you know this?' The boy asked.
'It is what I studied and practiced my whole life. It is the art of being happy by looking within for happiness.'
'You are here as an old man, alone. Does it work?'
'Yes. But that is enough. If you want to know more I will have to tell you tomorrow. I must go and get some food.'

The old man got up and took a hessian bag with him as he walked out of the door towards the direction of the road.

When the old man had gone the boy took out a pencil and a notebook and wrote down what the man had told him.

✳

The next morning the boy was once again woken by the

rays of sunlight reflecting off the walls and the shiny floor.

The old man was sitting still with his eyes closed facing the hills through the window. The boy watched him and became aware that the man seemed to radiate a peacefulness which brought the boys mind to a state of being very conscious of his thoughts. It was as if the old man was showing him something and he was inviting him to follow his example.

When the old man opened his eyes from looking out the window, as he had done the day before, he turned to the boy and spoke again.

'Every morning when you sit in stillness ask, Why am I here? The answer is to be happy inside. Then ask, Who am I? The answer is realised by seeing what you are not. I am not this, not that. I am consciousness. I am that I am, which is everything. I am that.'

∞

'These are the two questions which you should ask every day at the beginning of your day.' There was a pause almost as if he wanted the boy to remember.

∞

'The answer to Why am I here is this. It is to find the happiness which is inside you.' He paused again, once more so as if that the boy could remember what he had said.

∞

'The answer to the Who am I is this. You find out by finding out what you are not. You say you are not this and not that. You are not your thoughts. You are not a collection of thoughts which is called the ego.' He paused again as if to let the boy absorb what he had said.

∞

'What is really you is not your body. It is not your memories or your thoughts about the future. You are simply consciousness without thoughts.' He paused again.

∞

'What has always been there aware of all your thoughts is your consciousness. It is what sees without eyes, what hears without ears. That is what you are.' There was one last pause, the longest.

∞

'Seeing that you are this consciousness of everything which is the same as the consciousness of the universe is what we are. You must actually be it.

'How do you know this?' The boy asked.

'It is what I studied and practiced my whole life. It is the art of being happy by looking within for happiness.'

'You are here as an old man, alone. Does it work?'

46

'Yes. But that is enough. If you want to know more I will have to tell you tomorrow. I must go and get some food.'

The old man got up and took a hessian bag with him as he walked out of the door towards the direction of the road. He did not return.

When the old man had gone the boy took out a pencil and a notebook and wrote down what the man had told him.

Later he thought he heard a sound outside. He went out to see what it was with his oil lamp as it was dark.

He noticed a young man who had put his bag against a tree. He was sitting in a deep sleep.

He held the lamp up to look at the young man's face. When he held the lamp up, he noticed the skin of his own hands had skin creases of an old man.

SAGES

Like Groundhog Day, it can seem that repeated effort keeps on returning us to the same place. But with perseverance, eventually we see who we are and we are released.

The young woman woke and saw the poor light of the pre-dawn darkness. She turned and acknowledged the light again then she slipped out of bed.

She bathed then dressed and went to revive the embers of the fire from the previous night's cooking. She added small dry twigs, then small branches then laid three logs on the smoking logs.

After a breakfast of break and milk the young woman tidied and cleaned the two small rooms. She then began to make bread. Whilst kneading the bread she went outside to see what the day was like. She felt the cool air on her face and arms because clouds were still hiding the heat and light from the sun. She knew the heat of the day would slowly appear after two hours and after that, three people would arrive to collect loaves of bread for their day.

When the sun had set the young woman began to make the second batch of bread. Whilst kneading the bread she went outside to see what the day was like. She felt the warm air on her face and arms because of the heat still rising from the hot earth. She knew the cooler night air would slowly appear after two hours and after that, three people would arrive to collect loaves of bread for the next day.

When they had gone, she ate the bread she had made along with the vegetables and milk she had exchanged for loaves of bread. As the fire died down she fell asleep.

*

The young woman woke and saw the poor light of the pre-dawn darkness. She turned and acknowledged the light again then she slipped out of bed.

She bathed then dressed and went to revive the embers of the fire from the previous night's cooking. She added small dry twigs, then small branches then laid three logs on the smoking logs.

After a breakfast of break and milk the young woman tidied and cleaned the two small rooms. She then began to make bread. Whilst kneading the bread she went outside to see what the day was like. She felt the cool air on her face and arms because clouds were still hiding the heat and light from the sun. She knew the heat of the day would slowly appear after two hours and after that, three people would arrive to collect loaves of bread for their day

Whilst kneading the bread the young woman thought she heard a voice singing. She thought she had imagined it as no one came to this area of the land near the coast as it led to nowhere. But there is it was again. She thought she heard a young woman's voice talking or maybe even singing. She went outside and looked around but there was no one.

When the sun had set the young woman began to make the second batch of bread. Whilst kneading the bread she went outside to see what the day was like. She felt the warm air on her face and arms because of the heat still rising from the hot earth. She knew the cooler night air would slowly appear after two hours and after that, three people would arrive to collect loaves of bread for the next day.

When they had gone, she ate the bread she had made along with the vegetables and milk she had exchanged for loaves of bread. As the fire died down she fell asleep.

*

The young woman woke and saw the poor light of the pre-dawn darkness. She turned and acknowledged the light again then she slipped out of bed.

She bathed then dressed and went to revive the embers of the fire from the previous night's cooking. She added small dry twigs, then small branches then laid three logs on the smoking logs.

After a breakfast of break and milk the young woman tidied and cleaned the two small rooms. She then began to make bread. Whilst kneading the bread she went outside to see what the day was like. She felt the cool air on her face and arms because clouds were still hiding the heat and light from the sun. She knew the heat of the day would slowly appear after two hours and after that, three people would arrive to collect loaves of bread for their day.

Whilst kneading the bread the young woman thought she heard a voice singing. She thought she had imagined it as no one came to this area of the land near the coast as it led to nowhere. But there is it was again. She thought she heard a young woman's voice talking or maybe even singing. She went outside and looked around but there was no one.

She remembered this happened the day before at exactly the same time. There were no visitors to the area and certainly none she knew of. She could not work out where the young woman's voice was coming from or what it was that maybe sounded like a young woman's voice singing.

When the sun had set the young woman began to make the second batch of bread. Whilst kneading the bread she went outside to see what the day was like. She felt the warm air on her face and arms because of the heat still rising from the hot earth. She knew the cooler night air would slowly appear after two hours and after that, three people would arrive to collect loaves of bread for the next day.

When they had gone, she ate the bread she had made along with the vegetables and milk she had exchanged for loaves of bread. As the fire died down she fell asleep.

*

The young woman woke and saw the poor light of the pre-dawn darkness. She turned and acknowledged the light again then she slipped out of bed.

She bathed then dressed and went to revive the embers of the fire from the previous night's cooking. She added small dry twigs, then small branches then laid three logs on the smoking logs.

After a breakfast of break and milk the young woman tidied and cleaned the two small rooms. She then began to make bread. Whilst kneading the bread she went outside to see what the day was like. She felt the cool air on her face and arms because clouds were still hiding the heat and light from the sun. She knew the heat of the day would slowly appear after two hours and after that, three people would arrive to collect loaves of bread for their day.

Whilst kneading the bread the young woman thought she heard a voice singing. She thought she had imagined it as no one came to this area of the land near the coast as it led to nowhere. But there is it was again. She thought she heard a young woman's voice talking or maybe even singing. She went outside and looked around but there was no one.

She remembered this happened the day before at exactly the same time. There were no visitors to the area and certainly none she knew of. She could not work out where the young woman's voice was coming from or what it was that maybe sounded like a young woman's voice.

She went back to kneading the bread and this time the voice was louder. It was closer. It was in the room with her. She had begun singing. She immediately stopped. She did not usually sing.

When the sun had set the young woman began to make the second batch of bread. Whilst kneading the bread she went outside to see what the day was like. She felt the warm air on her face and arms because of the heat still rising from the hot earth. She knew the cooler night air would slowly appear after two hours and after that, three people would arrive to collect loaves of bread for the next day.

When they had gone, she ate the bread she had made

along with the vegetables and milk she had exchanged for loaves of bread. As the fire died down she fell asleep.

*

The young woman woke and saw the poor light of the pre-dawn darkness. She turned and acknowledged the light again then she slipped out of bed.

She bathed then dressed and went to revive the embers of the fire from the previous night's cooking. She added small dry twigs, then small branches then laid three logs on the smoking logs.

After a breakfast of break and milk the young woman tidied and cleaned the two small rooms. She then began to make bread. Whilst kneading the bread she went outside to see what the day was like. She felt the cool air on her face and arms because clouds were still hiding the heat and light from the sun. She knew the heat of the day would slowly appear after two hours and after that, three people would arrive to collect loaves of bread for their day.

Whilst kneading the bread the young woman thought she heard a voice singing. She thought she had imagined it as no one came to this area of the land near the coast as it led to nowhere. But there is it was again. She thought she heard a young woman's voice talking or maybe even singing. She went outside and looked around but there was no one.

She remembered this happened the day before at exactly the same time. There were no visitors to the area and certainly none she knew of. She could not work out

54

where the young woman's voice was coming from or what it was that maybe sounded like a young woman's voice.

She went back to kneading the bread and this time the voice was louder. It was closer. It was in the room with her. She had begun singing. She immediately stopped. She did not usually sing. But now, even though she stopped she could hear a voice singing. She felt very strange as if she was about to become ill so she went to lay down on the bed.

When the sun had set the young woman began to make the second batch of bread. Whilst kneading the bread she went outside to see what the day was like. She felt the warm air on her face and arms because of the heat still rising from the hot earth. She knew the cooler night air would slowly appear after two hours and after that, three people would arrive to collect loaves of bread for the next day.

When they had gone, she ate the bread she had made along with the vegetables and milk she had exchanged for loaves of bread. As the fire died down she fell asleep.

*

The young woman woke and saw the poor light of the pre-dawn darkness. She turned and acknowledged the light again then she slipped out of bed.

She bathed then dressed and went to revive the embers of the fire from the previous night's cooking. She added small dry twigs, then small branches then laid three logs on the smoking logs.

After a breakfast of break and milk the young woman tidied and cleaned the two small rooms. She then began to make bread. Whilst kneading the bread she went outside to see what the day was like. She felt the cool air on her face and arms because clouds were still hiding the heat and light from the sun. She knew the heat of the day would slowly appear after two hours and after that, three people would arrive to collect loaves of bread for their day.

Whilst kneading the bread the young woman thought she heard a voice singing. She thought she had imagined it as no one came to this area of the land near the coast as it led to nowhere. But there is it was again. She thought she heard a young woman's voice talking or maybe even singing. She went outside and looked around but there was no one.

She remembered this happened the day before at exactly the same time. There were no visitors to the area and certainly none she knew of. She could not work out where the young woman's voice was coming from or what it was that maybe sounded like a young woman's voice.

She went back to kneading the bread and this time the voice was louder. It was closer. It was in the room with her. She had begun singing. She immediately stopped. She did not usually sing. But now, even though she stopped she could hear a voice singing. She felt very strange as if she was about to become ill so she went to lay down on the bed.

The young woman was woken by knocking on the wooden door. She listened and there it was again. She got off the bed and gathered and smoothed out her clothes as she never had visitors. Nervously and fully prepared to defend her small dwelling against any intruder she opened the door.

At first she couldn't see the face of the figure who was silhouetted by light from the rising sun behind. The young woman saw that it was the figure of an older woman and then made out the face which had a gentle smile. She noticed immediately that the woman's smile was serene, unlike how she saw her own smile.

She beckoned her inside but the woman did not come in. Instead, she stood on the threshold of the dwelling.

'I am looking for a room for a night or two.'

'I don't have a spare room, just the floor of the kitchen. But I can make up a mattress and I have extra blankets and pillows.'

'This is kind as you don't even know me.

'What's your business here?'

'I am travelling to meet my sister in the south.'

'Then you are welcome to stay. I can make a bed for you.'

'This is kind of you.'

'This morning I have made some warm bread and there is some milk if you are thirsty.'

'This is kindness again.' The woman said, putting her shoulder bag on the stone floor.

The sun was setting and they got up to go inside the dwelling. When the sun had set the woman began to make the second batch of bread. Whilst kneading the bread she went outside to see what the day was like. She felt the warm air on her face and arms because of the heat still rising from the hot earth. She knew the cooler night air would slowly appear after two hours and after that, three people would arrive to collect loaves of bread for the next day.

When they had gone, the young woman sat with her as they ate the bread she had made along with the vegetables and milk she had exchanged for loaves of bread. As the fire died down they fell asleep in their beds.

*

The young woman woke and saw the poor light of the pre-dawn darkness. She turned and acknowledged the light again then she slipped out of bed.

She bathed then dressed and went to revive the embers of the fire from the previous night's cooking. She added small dry twigs, then small branches then laid three logs on the smoking logs.

Beside the makeshift bed lay with the woman's large shoulder bag. She thought she may have gone for a walk in the early morning cool air so she once again she waited for her to return.

After a breakfast of break and milk the young woman tidied and cleaned the two small rooms. She then began to make bread. Whilst kneading the bread she went outside to see what the day was like. She felt the cool air on her face and arms because clouds were still hiding the heat and light from the sun. She knew the heat of the day would slowly appear after two hours and after that, three people would arrive to collect loaves of bread for their day.

Whilst kneading the bread the young woman thought she heard a voice singing, just like the last few days. It was the same voice, the one she had heard before. But now it was not her singing. It was coming from outside the house. It was as if she was being called by someone outside.

She went outside and looked around but there was no one. Then she heard the voice singing again. It was coming from the back of the dwelling. She walked around and there sitting on one of several logs, looking into the distance was the woman. She was not singing and it was then that she realised that her own inner voice was calling her to see this woman.

The woman sat still with her eyes closed as the young woman came and sat opposite her.

She saw that the woman's face looked more serene than the day before when she had first met her. The young woman had a sense that the calmness and peace in the woman's face was very pure. She could only liken her serene state to the innocence of a flower or the face of a child.

She sat down opposite her and looked at her. As she did, she noticed her thoughts slowed down so much that there was only the occasional thought.

She was sitting being still with this woman and not thinking as much as usual. Several times she would suddenly be aware that she had been in a state she could not describe but which was very pleasant. It was neither sleep nor being in a trance, but it was so relaxed she wanted more of it. She felt she didn't want the woman to open her eyes. She felt she didn't want her to leave and go on her journey more south.

'Can you tell me how I can get happiness like you?'

'Happiness is not a Possession. What makes you think you don't have happiness?'

'I've lived here since my aunt died. She brought me up. I feel detached and not like everyone else. I am very serious about everything and everyone but I just can't seem to find happiness in myself like everyone else.'

'What makes you so sure they are happy?'

'I'm not sure, but they seem happier than me.'

'What you see on the outside is rarely what is going on in the inside because few know that our happiness is inside and even fewer know how to look inside to find it.'

'How do I look inside?'

'Knowing your self is a skill learnt like any other skill.' But is the most important one of your whole life.'

'How do I learn that skill?'

'If you are hungry enough, like a starving person, you can learn it.'

The sun was setting and so they got up to go inside the dwelling. When the sun had set the young woman began to make the second batch of bread.

Whilst kneading the bread she went outside to see what the day was like. She felt the warm air on her face and arms because of the heat still rising from the hot earth. She knew the cooler night air would slowly appear after two hours and after that, three people would arrive to collect loaves of bread for the next day.

When they had gone, the woman sat with her as they

ate the bread she had made along with the vegetables and milk she had exchanged for loaves of bread. As the fire died down they fell asleep in their beds.

*

The young woman woke and saw the poor light of the pre-dawn darkness. She turned and acknowledged the light again then she slipped out of bed.

She bathed then dressed and went to revive the embers of the fire from the previous night's cooking. She added small dry twigs, then small branches then laid three logs on the smoking logs.

Beside the makeshift bed lay with the woman's large shoulder bag. She thought she may have gone for a walk in the early morning cool air so she waited for her to return.

After a breakfast of break and milk the young woman tidied and cleaned the two small rooms. She then began to make bread. Whilst kneading the bread she went outside to see what the day was like. She felt the cool air on her face and arms because clouds were still hiding the heat and light from the sun. She knew the heat of the day would slowly appear after two hours and after that, three people would arrive to collect loaves of bread for their day.

Whilst kneading the bread the young woman thought she heard a voice singing, just like the last few days. It was the same voice, the one she had heard before. But it was not her singing. It was coming from outside the house. It was as if she was being called by someone outside. She went outside and looked around but there was no one. Then she heard the voice singing again. It was coming from the back of the dwelling. She walked around and there sitting on one of several logs, looking into the distance was the woman. She was not singing and it was then that she again realised that her own inner voice was calling her to see this woman.

The woman sat still with her eyes closed as the young woman came and sat opposite her.

She saw that the woman's face looked more serene than the day before when she had first met her. The young woman had a sense that the calmness and peace in the woman's face was very pure. She could only liken her serene state to the innocence of a flower or the face of a child.

She sat down opposite her and looked at her. As she did, she noticed her thoughts slowed down so much that there was only the occasional thought.

She was sitting being still with this woman and not thinking as much as usual. Several times she would suddenly be aware that she had been in a state she could not describe but which was very pleasant. It was neither sleep nor being in a trance, but it was so relaxed she wanted more of it. She felt she didn't want the woman to open her eyes. She felt she didn't want her to leave and go on her journey more south.

'Can you tell me how I can get happiness like you?'

'As we saw yesterday, happiness is not a Possession. You may have looked at acquiring money, things, power, influence or knowledge to make you happy. You may have looked at having all of these possessions to make you happy. But these will make you bored and you will endlessly keep going onto the next best thing.'

∞

'Possessions lead to fear of their use and loss. Fear and loss make us think we will be happier if we can more securely possess them, so an endless pursuit begins. Loss anxiety makes us try harder to possess what does not even make us happy.'

∞

'Don't be misled by beauty because Beauty is something recognised outside, happiness is always inside. Beauty is derived from the senses, happiness is revealed inside. Beauty is a synthesis of fine thinking, happiness is simply being in the heart with no thoughts.'

∞

'There is no relationship between any form of possession and happiness. How do we know this? A powerful wealthy influential person will always have loss anxiety about their securities. They cannot be as happy as the person who has found happiness inside. Seeing that acquiring things, money, power, influence or knowledge does not make you happy, there is only one place left to look for happiness. Inside.'

The sun was setting and they got up to go inside the

dwelling. When the sun had set the young woman began to make the second batch of bread.

Whilst kneading the bread she went outside to see what the day was like. She felt the warm air on her face and arms because of the heat still rising from the hot earth. She knew the cooler night air would slowly appear after two hours and after that, three people would arrive to collect loaves of bread for the next day.

When they had gone, the woman sat with her as they ate the bread she had made along with the vegetables and milk she had exchanged for loaves of bread. As the fire died down they fell asleep in their beds.

✻

The young woman woke and saw the poor light of the pre-dawn darkness. She turned and acknowledged the light again then she slipped out of bed.

She bathed then dressed and went to revive the embers of the fire from the previous night's cooking. She added small dry twigs, then small branches then laid three logs on the smoking logs.

After a breakfast of break and milk the young woman tidied and cleaned the two small rooms. She then began to make bread. Whilst kneading the bread she went outside to see what the day was like. She felt the cool air on her face and arms because clouds were still hiding the heat and light from the sun. She knew the heat of the day would slowly appear after two hours and after that, three people would arrive to collect loaves of bread for their day.

After the three people had collected their loaves the young woman went around to the back of the house where the woman was sitting the day before.

The woman was sitting still with her eyes closed as the young woman came and sat opposite her.

She saw once again that the woman's face looked more serene than when she had first met her. The young woman had a sense that the calmness and peace in the woman's face was very pure. Again, she could only liken her serene state to the innocence of a flower or the face of a child.

Sitting down opposite her and looking at her, she noticed her thoughts slowed down so much that there was only the occasional thought. She was sitting being still with this woman and not thinking as much as usual.

Several times she would suddenly be aware that she had been in state she could not describe but which was very pleasant. It was neither sleep nor being in a trance, but it was so relaxed she wanted more of it.

She felt she didn't want the woman to open her eyes. She felt she didn't want her to leave and go on her journey more south. She too closed her eyes.

Some time after she opened her eyes, she saw the woman also open her eyes and was not at all surprised to see the young woman sitting opposite her.

'What else can you say about happiness?' The young woman asked.

'To be happy you need to see you can't acquire it by adding something to yourself. Instead, see that you have to remove something about you. Get rid of your belief that you can acquire happiness by seeing you already have it.'

∞

'Happiness is seen by getting rid of searching for happiness because it is already inside you.'

∞

'Happiness is seen by getting rid of looking outside of you for happiness.'

∞

'Happiness is seen by getting rid of thinking security of any kind will make you happy.'

∞

'Happiness is seen by constant effort to be happy.'

The sun was setting and they got up to go inside the dwelling. When the sun had set the young woman began to make the second batch of bread. Whilst kneading the bread she went outside to see what the day was like. She felt the warm air on her face and arms because of the heat still rising from the hot earth. She knew the cooler night air would slowly appear after two hours and after that, three people would arrive to collect loaves of bread for the next day.

When they had gone, the woman sat with her as they

ate the bread she had made along with the vegetables and milk she had exchanged for loaves of bread. As the fire died down they fell asleep in their beds.

*

The young woman woke and saw the poor light of the pre-dawn darkness. She turned and acknowledged the light again then she slipped out of bed.

She bathed then dressed and went to revive the embers of the fire from the previous night's cooking. She added small dry twigs, then small branches then laid three logs on the smoking logs.

After a breakfast of break and milk the young woman tidied and cleaned the two small rooms. She then began to make bread. Whilst kneading the bread she went outside to see what the day was like. She felt the cool air on her face and arms because clouds were still hiding the heat and light from the sun. She knew the heat of the day would slowly appear after two hours and after that, three people would arrive to collect loaves of bread for their day.

After the three people had collected their loaves the young woman went around to the back of the house where the woman was sitting the day before. The woman was sitting still with her eyes closed as the young woman came and sat opposite her.

She saw once again that the woman's face looked more serene than when she had first met her. The young woman had a sense that the calmness and peace in the woman's face was very pure. Again, she could only liken her serene state to the innocence of a flower or the face of a child.

Sitting down opposite her and looking at her, she noticed her thoughts slowed down so much that there was only the occasional thought. She was sitting being still with this woman and not thinking as much as usual.

Several times she would suddenly be aware that she had been in state she could not describe but which was very pleasant. It was neither sleep nor being in a trance, but it was so relaxed she wanted more of it.

She felt she didn't want the woman to open her eyes. She felt she didn't want her to leave and go on her journey more south. She too closed her eyes.

Some time after she opened her eyes, she saw the woman also open her eyes and was not at all surprised to see the young woman sitting opposite her.

'Why is it so difficult to be happy?' The young woman asked.

'There are three things we don't see. The first is that to access happiness we have to get rid of thinking it is outside. Like light is always here from the sun but we may be busy looking at something else; we only need to turn inside to see our happiness.'

∞

'We may not be able to be happy all the time but our happiness is always here inside us. Your happiness depends on seeing your happiness is already inside you and is not something new which can be acquired from outside.'

∞

'The second is that you can't actually ever be happy tomorrow, only today. You can only be happy today, in the present, right now, so give up the search in the future, so you can see it now. Happiness is inside and we can only be happy right now today.

∞

'The third is that to be happy now, you have to be happy with what you have and have no want. To be happy with what you are and what you have is to be happy with just sufficient. Sufficient is what is enough. Enough for how long? Well today is how long.'

The sun was setting and they got up to go inside the dwelling. When the sun had set the young woman began to make the second batch of bread. Whilst kneading the bread she went outside to see what the day was like. She felt the warm air on her face and arms because of the heat still rising from the hot earth. She knew the cooler night air would slowly appear after two hours and after that, three people would arrive to collect loaves of bread for the next day.

When they had gone, the woman sat with her as they ate the bread she had made along with the vegetables and milk she had exchanged for loaves of bread. As the fire died down they fell asleep in their beds.

*

The young woman woke and saw the poor light of the pre-dawn darkness. She turned and acknowledged the light again then she slipped out of bed.

She bathed then dressed and went to revive the embers of the fire from the previous night's cooking. She added small dry twigs, then small branches then laid three logs on the smoking logs.

Beside the makeshift bed lay with the woman's large shoulder bag. She thought she was probably sitting again outside at the back of the dwelling.

After a breakfast of break and milk the young woman tidied and cleaned the two small rooms. She then began to make bread. Whilst kneading the bread she went outside to see what the day was like. She felt the cool air on her face and arms because clouds were still hiding the heat and light from the sun. She knew the heat of the day would slowly appear after two hours and after that, three people would arrive to collect loaves of bread for their day.

After the young woman had tidied and cleaned the two small rooms she began to make some bread. Whilst kneading the bread the young woman thought she heard a voice singing, just like the last few days. It was the same voice, the one she had heard before. But now, once more, it was not her singing. It was coming from outside the house.

She went outside and looked around but there was no one. Then she heard the voice singing again. Once again it was coming from the back of the dwelling. She walked around and there sitting on one of several logs looking into the distance was the woman.

The woman sat still with her eyes closed as the young woman came and sat opposite her.

She saw once again that the woman's face looked more serene than when she had first met her. The young woman had a sense that the calmness and peace in the woman's face was very pure. She could only liken her serene state to the innocence of a flower or the face of a child.

She sat down opposite her and looked at her. As she did, she noticed her thoughts slowed down so much that there was only the occasional thought.

She was sitting being still with this woman and not thinking as much as usual. Several times she would suddenly be aware that she had been in state she could not describe but which was very pleasant. It was neither sleep nor being in a trance, but it was so relaxed she wanted more of it. She felt she didn't want the woman to open her eyes. She felt she didn't want her to leave and go on her journey more south.

Then as if in slow motion the woman opened her eyes and was not at all surprised to see the young woman sitting opposite her.

'When can I be happy like you?

'When you see you are as happy as you can be today without wanting anything, you have found happiness.'

∞

'When you are free from pain and free from desiring

71

pleasure, you are happy. Possessions lead to fear of their use and loss.'

∞

'When you see this you see you have no want.'

∞

'When you see you have no want you cannot be happier.'

∞

'With no want you are happy'

∞

'Do you know a person with no want?'

∞

'The easiest way to make yourself an exile from your happiness is to start thinking about the past or what you want in the future.'

The sun was setting and they got up to go inside the dwelling. When the sun had set the young woman began to make the second batch of bread. Whilst kneading the bread she went outside to see what the day was like. She felt the warm air on her face and arms because of the heat still rising from the hot earth. She knew the cooler night air would slowly appear after two hours and after that, three people would arrive to collect loaves of bread for the next day.

When they had gone, the woman sat with her as they ate the bread she had made along with the vegetables and milk she had exchanged for loaves of bread. As the fire died down they fell asleep in their beds.

*

The young woman woke and saw the poor light of the pre-dawn darkness. She turned and acknowledged the light again then she slipped out of bed.

She bathed then dressed and went to revive the embers of the fire from the previous night's cooking. She added small dry twigs, then small branches then laid three logs on the smoking logs.

After a breakfast of break and milk the young woman tidied and cleaned the two small rooms. She then began to make bread. Whilst kneading the bread she went outside to see what the day was like. She felt the cool air on her face and arms because clouds were still hiding the heat and light from the sun. She knew the heat of the day would slowly appear after two hours and after that, three people would arrive to collect loaves of bread for their day.

After the three people had collected their loaves the young woman went around to the back of the house where the woman was sitting the day before.

The woman was sitting still with her eyes closed as

the young woman came and sat opposite her.

She saw once again that the woman's face looked more serene than when she had first met her. The young woman had a sense that the calmness and peace in the woman's face was very pure. Again, she could only liken her serene state to the innocence of a flower or the face of a child.

Sitting down opposite her and looking at her, she noticed her thoughts slowed down so much that there was only the occasional thought. She was sitting being still with this woman and not thinking as much as usual.

Several times she would suddenly be aware that she had been in state she could not describe but which was very pleasant. It was neither sleep nor being in a trance, but it was so relaxed she wanted more of it. She felt she didn't want the woman to open her eyes. She felt she didn't want her to leave and go on her journey more south. She too closed her eyes.

Then as if in slow motion the woman opened her eyes and was not at all surprised to see the young woman sitting opposite her.

'How come you are so happy?'

'We are not born unhappy but our circumstances make us unhappy, so we try to find the happiness we know is inside. This is our nature. But we make the mistake of looking for happiness outside rather than inside.'

'Why do we look outside rather than inside?'

'People and organisations are more interested in you not looking inside. They want you to depend on them for your happiness.'

∞

'Our happiness is our self which is the same as everything in the Universe and no different from it.'

∞

'Religions point to seeing our inner self as our higher power inside us or as God. Most simply this is consciousness of 'I am.' This can be seen in the words from the east and the west over the last three thousand years.'

∞

'Let us demystify religions.'

∞

'What is really you is not your body. It is not your memories or your thoughts about the future. You are simply consciousness without thoughts.'

∞

'What has always been there aware of all your thoughts is your consciousness. It is what sees without eyes, what hears without ears. That is what you are.' There was one last pause, the longest.

∞

'Seeing that you are this consciousness, it has to be the same as all consciousness. This has to be the consciousness of everything, which is the same as the consciousness of the universe. You eventually see this is in truth what you are. But you must actually be it.'

∞

'We ask what the mystery of life is. Why are we here? What are we here for? The answer is simple. We are only here to be happy.'

∞

'Religions know we prefer mystery to reality. The ancients knew it.'

∞

'The ancient civilisations knew it. They knew that happiness was inside. In Judaism, when Moses asked God for his name he answered, "I Am That I Am. Thus shalt you say unto the children of Israel, I Am has sent me to you." Jehovah means I am. So knowing the self, God is known as they are taken to be the same.'

∞

'The Pashupati Seal is a soapstone seal discovered in the Indus Valley Civilisation. It is estimated to have been carved around 2350 BC and is thought to be the earliest prototype of the God Shiva. The seal shows a seated cross-legged figure in the yogic lotus meditation posture with arms pointing downwards. It is important because it is one of the first communications from our ancient ancestors which reflects the stillness of silently looking inwards.'

∞

'In Hinduism the mind is helped to look inwards by, "Netti Netti," from the Brihadaranyaka Upanishad written around 800 BC, meaning, "Neither this neither this," which helps the mind to constantly disidentify with anything other than that which is everything.'

∞

'One of the ancient Greek's key instructions, "Know the self," was written on the portals of their most important temple, the Temple of Apollo in Delphi.'

∞

'In the Hebrew Bible or the Tanaka, in Psalm 46, God is assumed to be inside, "Be still and know that I am God."

∞

'And again in Christianity in Luke 17, it says, "The

kingdom of God is within you." Do you see it?'

∞

'Even Shakespeare pointed man strongly inside, "This above all-to thine own self be true."

∞

'In the 8th century, an Indian guru, Adi Shankara, said, "The fool takes the reflection of the sun in the water of a pot to be the sun; the wise man eliminates pot, water, and reflection and knows the sun in the sky as it really is, single and unaffected, but illuminating all three. In the same way the fool through error and misperception, identifies himself with the ego and its reflected light experienced through the medium of the intellect. The wise and discriminating man eliminates body, intellect, and reflected light of consciousness and probes deeply into his real Self which illuminates all three while remaining uniform in the ether of the heart. Thereby he realises the eternal witness which is absolute knowledge, illuminating all three."

∞

'All of this was most clearly summarised by another Indian Guru, Ramana Maharshi when he said in 1937, "Your duty is to be and not to be this or that. I AM that I AM, sums up the whole truth. The method is summarised in, Be still. What does stillness mean? It means, destroy yourself. Because any form or shape is the cause of trouble. Give up the notion that "I am so and so."

∞

'So you see, they all say that happiness is inside. We have to be that consciousness not just in the morning when we sit still. But gradually we become that consciousness 'I Am' more and more throughout the day. We surrender to it. We surrender our Self to the Universe. Then we become it.'

The sun was setting and they got up to go inside the dwelling. When the sun had set the young woman began to make the second batch of bread. Whilst kneading the bread she went outside to see what the day was like. She felt the warm air on her face and arms because of the heat still rising from the hot earth. She knew the cooler night air would slowly appear after two hours and after that, three people would arrive to collect loaves of bread for the next day.

When they had gone, the woman sat with her as they ate the bread she had made along with the vegetables and milk she had exchanged for loaves of bread. As the fire died down they fell asleep in their beds.

＊

The young woman woke and saw the poor light of the pre-dawn darkness. She turned and acknowledged the light again then she slipped out of bed.

She bathed then dressed and went to revive the

embers of the fire from the previous night's cooking. She added small dry twigs, then small branches then laid three logs on the smoking logs.

After a breakfast of break and milk the young woman tidied and cleaned the two small rooms. She then began to make bread. Whilst kneading the bread she went outside to see what the day was like. She felt the cool air on her face and arms because clouds were still hiding the heat and light from the sun. She knew the heat of the day would slowly appear after two hours and after that, three people would arrive to collect loaves of bread for their day.

After the three people had collected their loaves the young woman went around to the back of the house where the woman was sitting the day before.

The woman was sitting still with her eyes closed as the young woman came and sat opposite her.

She saw once again that the woman's face looked more serene than when she had first met her. The young woman had a sense that the calmness and peace in the woman's face was very pure. Again she could only liken her serene state to the innocence of a flower or the face of a child.

Sitting down opposite her and looking at her, she noticed her thoughts slowed down so much that there was only the occasional thought. She was sitting being still with this woman and not thinking as much as usual.

Several times she would suddenly be aware that she had been in state she could not describe but which was very pleasant. It was neither sleep nor being in a trance, but it was so relaxed she wanted more of it. She felt she didn't want the woman to open her eyes. She felt she didn't want her to leave and go on her journey more south. She too closed her eyes.

Some time after she opened her eyes, she saw the woman also open her eyes and was not at all surprised to see the young woman sitting opposite her.

'What is the meaning of our life? Asked the young woman.

'This is reality for me.' Said the woman. 'Sitting in stillness in happiness inside.

'I'm not sure I get that.'

'Do you know who you really are?'

'I'm just me, a simple householder.'

'You are not just a simple householder.'

'By seeing what we are not we see who we really are.'

'The world which we believe is real, is only the one we experience with all our senses in our body. It is what we believe is real after we have processed all the information with our thoughts in our brain.'

'I don't understand.'

'Although we believe that the world we experience is reality, we have just fooled ourselves with our thinking. When you close your eyes and let your inner self just be without thoughts, you see that thoughts keep on coming and going. It is then you see you can look down on thoughts, like looking from high up on a mountain down onto a river below.'

The sun was setting and they got up to go inside the dwelling. When the sun had set the young woman began to make the second batch of bread. Whilst kneading the bread she went outside to see what the day was like. She felt the warm air on her face and arms because of the heat still rising from the hot earth. She knew the cooler night air would slowly appear after two hours and after that, three people would arrive to collect loaves of bread for the next day.

When they had gone, the woman sat with her as they ate the bread she had made along with the vegetables and milk she had exchanged for loaves of bread. As the fire died down they fell asleep in their beds.

✳

The young woman woke and saw the poor light of the pre-dawn darkness. She turned and acknowledged the light again then she slipped out of bed.

She bathed then dressed and went to revive the embers of the fire from the previous night's cooking. She added small dry twigs, then small branches then laid three logs on the smoking logs.

After a breakfast of break and milk the young woman tidied and cleaned the two small rooms. She then began to make bread. Whilst kneading the bread she went outside to see what the day was like. She felt the cool air on her face and arms because clouds were still hiding the heat and light from the sun. She knew the heat of the day would slowly appear after two hours and after that, three people would arrive to collect loaves of bread for their day.

After the three people had collected their loaves

the young woman went around to the back of the house where the woman was sitting the day before.

The woman was sitting still with her eyes closed as the young woman came and sat opposite her.

She saw once again that the woman's face looked more serene than when she had first met her. The young woman had a sense that the calmness and peace in the woman's face was very pure. Again, she could only liken her serene state to the innocence of a flower or the face of a child.

Sitting down opposite her and looking at her, she noticed her thoughts slowed down so much that there was only the occasional thought. She was sitting being still with this woman and not thinking as much as usual.

Several times she would suddenly be aware that she had been in state she could not describe but which was very pleasant. It was neither sleep nor being in a trance, but it was so relaxed she wanted more of it. She felt she didn't want the woman to open her eyes. She felt she didn't want her to leave and go on her journey more south. She too closed her eyes.

Some time after she opened her eyes, she saw the woman also open her eyes and was not at all surprised to see the young woman sitting opposite her.

'I looked at what you said yesterday about me being consciousness and not just being my thoughts.'

'Seeing our goal is inner stillness, we try to use thinking to find it but we can only find our stillness by being still, not by thinking about it.'

∞

'When we look inside at 'Who are we?' we become conscious we are not thought.'

'It is a surprise to discover that you are not your thoughts, which through reflection seem like imposters.'

∞

'We are taught and programmed to believe we are a bundle of thoughts called the ego.'

∞

'But in meditation you see you are not just a bundle of thoughts.'

∞

'When you stay with this, you begin to see consciousness comes before thought. Consciousness is always here. Thought comes and goes.'

∞

'In meditation you see you are consciousness which is not a thought but is what creates thought. This is what our ancestors meant by the expression, I am.'

∞

'There is no more mystery.'

∞

'There is no more misery about our thinking.'

∞

'In wanting to see what we are, it is essential to ask and find out what we are not.'

∞

'We think we are our memories, but these are just thoughts, so if we believe this, we can easily take ourselves to be what we are not. We may think we are what we imagine in the future but this is just thought and is not what we are now.'

∞

'In asking what you are and what you are not, you see you are not your thoughts but consciousness, which is responsible for thoughts.'

∞

'When something is made up it has no authenticity; just as you always know when an actor is acting.'

∞

'The same mistaken authenticity is obvious when

our ignorance of believing we are the ego is uncovered.'

∞

'You can see what you are is consciousness of stillness inside you.'

∞

'Consciousness of inner stillness lets us see our inner self is stillness.'

∞

'Consciousness of inner stillness lets us see that our inner self is our natural happiness.'

∞

'Our answer to what we are is I am just 'I am,' the consciousness we all have of inner stillness.'

The sun was setting and they got up to go inside the dwelling. When the sun had set the young woman began to make the second batch of bread. Whilst kneading the bread she went outside to see what the day was like. She felt the warm air on her face and arms because of the heat still rising from the hot earth. She knew the cooler night air would slowly appear after two hours and after that, three people would arrive to collect loaves of bread for the next day.

When they had gone, the woman sat with her as they ate the bread she had made along with the vegetables and milk she had exchanged for loaves of bread. As the fire died down they fell asleep in their beds.

✳

The young woman woke and saw the poor light of the pre-dawn darkness. She turned and acknowledged the light again then she slipped out of bed.

She bathed then dressed and went to revive the embers of the fire from the previous night's cooking. She added small dry twigs, then small branches then laid three logs on the smoking logs.

After a breakfast of break and milk the young woman tidied and cleaned the two small rooms. She then began to make bread. Whilst kneading the bread she went outside to see what the day was like. She felt the cool air on her face and arms because clouds were still hiding the heat and light from the sun. She knew the heat of the day would slowly appear after two hours and after that, three people would arrive to collect loaves of bread for their day.

After the three people had collected their loaves the young woman went around to the back of the house where the woman was sitting the day before.

The woman was sitting still with her eyes closed as the young woman came and sat opposite her.

She saw once again that the woman's face looked more serene than when she had first met her. The young woman had a sense that the calmness and peace in the

87

woman's face was very pure. Again, she could only liken her serene state to the innocence of a flower or the face of a child.

Sitting down opposite her and looking at her, she noticed her thoughts slowed down so much that there was only the occasional thought. She was sitting being still with this woman and not thinking as much as usual.

Several times she would suddenly be aware that she had been in state she could not describe but which was very pleasant. It was neither sleep nor being in a trance, but it was so relaxed she wanted more of it. She felt she didn't want the woman to open her eyes. She felt she didn't want her to leave and go on her journey more south. She too closed her eyes.

Some time after she opened her eyes, she saw the woman also open her eyes and was not at all surprised to see the young woman sitting opposite her.

'How do you meditate?'

'There is not one way to meditate. But there is only one final pathway.'

∞

'There are no techniques to meditate. But there are different levels of attainment in meditation.'

∞

'What we desire to be happy is to stop thoughts, to let us experience our stillness.'

∞

'To meditate we need to withdraw inside to experience this one thing only.'

∞

'There are different levels of attainment in meditation we may be able to experience. Our level of attainment may be different at different times for each of us.'

∞

'If we find it difficult to start by withdrawing inside to see what we are and what we are not, we can turn inwards and gain some control of our mind, our thinking, by tethering it to one thing by following our breathing. It is controlling our mind.'

∞

'Next, we can turn inwards, tethering our mind by repeating a silent sound, a mantra.'

∞

'Meditation shows us we seem conditioned to keep on having thoughts instead of just being still without thoughts.'

∞

'Meditation is mind control, repeatedly stopping thoughts to let us be this inner stillness. The battle resumes every time we meditate. It requires effort. It requires one-pointedness. You need to keep the main aim the main aim.'

∞

'The more we meditate, the more we see thoughts are not us and so the battle of our consciousness against them becomes more effective.'

∞

'To be conscious of what we are as stillness is all we need to do. This consciousness of 'I am' is all we can be.'

∞

'We do not add anything to us to meditate. It is removal. We remove what is not us . . . thought. The reward is the indescribable conscious happiness of stillness.'

∞

'Each time you sit to meditate, ask yourself 'Why am I here?' The answer is 'Only to be happy.' Then ask yourself 'Who you are?' You will see that you are consciousness, not thought. The answers are found inside by being still.'

∞

'The method, path and goal of meditation are contained in the simple statement,' "Be still and know that I am That."

∞

'In other words, searching and seeing inner stillness with no thought is the method. Being conscious of 'I Am' is the only truth. It is all you can be. When you are this you are fully conscious and blissfully happy.'

The sun was setting and they got up to go inside the dwelling. When the sun had set the young woman began to make the second batch of bread. Whilst kneading the bread she went outside to see what the day was like. She felt the warm air on her face and arms because of the heat still rising from the hot earth. She knew the cooler night air would slowly appear after two hours and after that, three people would arrive to collect loaves of bread for the next day.

When they had gone, the woman sat with her as they ate the bread she had made along with the vegetables and milk she had exchanged for loaves of bread. As the fire died down they fell asleep in their beds.

＊

The young woman woke and saw the poor light of the pre-dawn darkness. She turned and acknowledged the light again then she slipped out of bed.

She bathed then dressed and went to revive the embers of the fire from the previous night's cooking. She added small dry twigs, then small branches then laid three logs on the smoking logs.

After a breakfast of break and milk the young woman tidied and cleaned the two small rooms. She then began to make bread. Whilst kneading the bread she went outside to see what the day was like. She felt the cool air on her face and arms because clouds were still hiding the heat and light from the sun. She knew the heat of the day would slowly appear after two hours and after that, three people would arrive to collect loaves of bread for their day.

After the three people had collected their loaves the young woman went around to the back of the house where the woman was sitting the day before.

The woman was sitting still with her eyes closed as the young woman came and sat opposite her.

She saw once again that the woman's face looked more serene than when she had first met her. The young woman had a sense that the calmness and peace in the woman's face was very pure. Again, she could only liken her serene state to the innocence of a flower or the face of a child.

Sitting down opposite her and looking at her, she noticed her thoughts slowed down so much that there was only the occasional thought. She was sitting being still with this woman and not thinking as much as usual.

Several times she would suddenly be aware that she had been in state she could not describe but which was very pleasant. It was neither sleep nor being in a trance, but it was so relaxed she wanted more of it. She felt she didn't want the woman to open her eyes. She felt she didn't want her to leave and go on her journey more south. She too closed her eyes.

Some time after she opened her eyes, she saw the woman also open her eyes and was not at all surprised to see the young woman sitting opposite her. After some time the woman spoke.

'You have found your happiness. The old you has been burnt to nothing by the fire of happiness. There are no words for the bliss of stillness.'

The sun was setting and they got up to go inside the dwelling. When the sun had set the young woman began to make the second batch of bread. Whilst kneading the bread she went outside to see what the day was like. She felt the warm air on her face and arms because of the heat still rising from the hot earth. She knew the cooler night air would slowly appear after two hours and after that, three people would arrive to collect loaves of bread for the next day.

When they had gone, the woman sat with her as they ate the bread she had made along with the vegetables and milk she had exchanged for loaves of bread. As the fire died down they fell asleep in their beds.

*

The young woman woke and saw the poor light of the pre-dawn darkness. She turned and acknowledged the light again then she slipped out of bed.

She bathed then dressed and went to revive the embers of the fire from the previous night's cooking. She added small dry twigs, then small branches then laid three logs on the smoking logs.

After a breakfast of break and milk the young woman tidied and cleaned the two small rooms. She then began to make bread. Whilst kneading the bread she went outside to see what the day was like. She felt the cool air on her face and arms because clouds were still hiding the heat and light from the sun. She knew the heat of the day would slowly appear after two hours and after that, three people would arrive to collect loaves of bread for their day.

After the three people had collected their loaves the young woman went around to the back of the house where the woman was sitting the day before.

The woman was sitting still with her eyes closed as the young woman came and sat opposite her.

She saw once again that the woman's face looked more serene than when she had first met her. The young woman had a sense that the calmness and peace in the woman's face was very pure. Again she could only liken her serene state to the innocence of a flower or the face of a child.

Sitting down opposite her and looking at her, she noticed her thoughts slowed down so much that there was only the occasional thought. She was sitting being still with this woman and not thinking as much as usual.

Several times she would suddenly be aware that she had almost been in state she could not describe but which was very pleasant. It was neither sleep nor being in a trance, but it was so relaxed she wanted more of it. She felt she didn't want the woman to open her eyes. She felt she didn't want her to leave and go on her journey more south. She too closed her eyes.

Some time after she opened her eyes, she saw the woman also open her eyes and was not at all surprised to see the young woman sitting opposite her.

'Does solitude help to be happy?'

'Yes. Solitude is an attitude. Solitude lets us detach from the distractions of the world.'

∞

'Solitude lets us detach from the distractions of the world, to experience happiness inside.'

∞

'Seeing our happiness is inside, we begin to spend more time in solitude and also with those whose view of the world is like ours.'

∞

'Detachment is separating our processes from other people's processes whilst still having a relationship.'

The sun was setting and they got up to go inside the

dwelling. When the sun had set the young woman began to make the second batch of bread. Whilst kneading the bread she went outside to see what the day was like. She felt the warm air on her face and arms because of the heat still rising from the hot earth. She knew the cooler night air would slowly appear after two hours and after that, three people would arrive to collect loaves of bread for the next day.

When they had gone, the woman sat with her as they ate the bread she had made along with the vegetables and milk she had exchanged for loaves of bread. As the fire died down they fell asleep in their beds.

*

The young woman woke and saw the poor light of the pre-dawn darkness. She turned and acknowledged the light again then she slipped out of bed.

She bathed then dressed and went to revive the embers of the fire from the previous night's cooking. She added small dry twigs, then small branches then laid three logs on the smoking logs.

After a breakfast of break and milk the young woman tidied and cleaned the two small rooms. She then began to make bread. Whilst kneading the bread she went outside to see what the day was like. She felt the cool air on her face and arms because clouds were still hiding the heat and light from the sun. She knew the heat of the day would slowly appear after two hours and after that, three people would arrive to collect loaves of bread for their day.

After the three people had collected their loaves the young woman went around to the back of the house where the woman was sitting the day before.

The woman was sitting still with her eyes closed as the young woman came and sat opposite her.

She saw once again that the woman's face looked more serene than when she had first met her. The young woman had a sense that the calmness and peace in the woman's face was very pure. Again, she could only liken her serene state to the innocence of a flower or the face of a child.

Sitting down opposite her and looking at her, she noticed her thoughts slowed down so much that there was only the occasional thought. She was sitting being still with this woman and not thinking as much as usual.

Several times she would suddenly be aware that she had almost been in state she could not describe but which was very pleasant. It was neither sleep nor being in a trance, but it was so relaxed she wanted more of it.

She felt she didn't want the woman to open her eyes. She felt she didn't want her to leave and go on her journey more south. She too closed her eyes.

Some time after she opened her eyes, she saw the woman also open her eyes and was not at all surprised to see the young woman sitting opposite her.

'What is the most important things about practice?'

'Try and be more and more conscious of 'I am' so that it is your default consciousness. Be one pointed in concentrating on this.'

∞

'Keep the Main Aim the Main Aim.'

∞

The sun was setting and they got up to go inside the dwelling. When the sun had set the young woman began to make the second batch of bread. Whilst kneading the bread she went outside to see what the day was like. She felt the warm air on her face and arms because of the heat still rising from the hot earth. She knew the cooler night air would slowly appear after two hours and after that, three people would arrive to collect loaves of bread for the next day.

When they had gone, the woman sat with her as they ate the bread she had made along with the vegetables and milk she had exchanged for loaves of bread. As the fire died down they fell asleep in their beds.

*

The young woman woke and saw the poor light of the pre-dawn darkness. She turned and acknowledged the light again then she slipped out of bed.

She bathed then dressed and went to revive the embers of the fire from the previous night's cooking. She added small dry twigs, then small branches then laid three logs on the smoking logs.

After a breakfast of break and milk the young woman tidied and cleaned the two small rooms. She then began to make bread. Whilst kneading the bread she went outside to see what the day was like. She felt the cool air on her face and arms because clouds were still hiding the heat and light from the sun. She knew the heat of the day would slowly appear after two hours and after that, three people would arrive to collect loaves of bread for their day.

After the three people had collected their loaves the young woman went around to the back of the house where the woman was sitting the day before.

The woman was sitting still with her eyes closed as the young woman came and sat opposite her.

She saw once again that the woman's face looked more serene than when she had first met her. The young woman had a sense that the calmness and peace in the woman's face was very pure. Again, she could only liken her serene state to the innocence of a flower or the face of a child.

Sitting down opposite her and looking at her she noticed her thoughts slowed down so much that there was only the occasional thought. She was sitting being still with this woman and not thinking as much as usual.

Several times she would suddenly be aware that she had been in state she could not describe but which was very pleasant. It was neither sleep nor being in a trance, but it was so relaxed she wanted more of it. She felt she didn't want the woman to open her eyes. She felt she didn't want her to leave and go on her journey more south. She too closed her eyes.

Some time after she opened her eyes, she saw the woman also open her eyes and was not at all surprised to see the young woman sitting opposite her. After some time the woman spoke.

'There are no words for stillness.'

The sun was setting and they got up to go inside the dwelling. When the sun had set the young woman began to make the second batch of bread. Whilst kneading the bread she went outside to see what the day was like. She felt the warm air on her face and arms because of the heat still rising from the hot earth. She knew the cooler night air would slowly appear after two hours and after that, three people would arrive to collect loaves of bread for the next day.

When they had gone, the woman sat with her as they ate the bread she had made along with the vegetables and milk she had exchanged for loaves of bread. As the fire died down they fell asleep in their beds.

✱

The young woman woke and saw the poor light of the pre-dawn darkness. She turned and acknowledged the light again then she slipped out of bed.

She bathed then dressed and went to revive the embers of the fire from the previous night's cooking. She added small dry twigs, then small branches then laid three logs on the smoking logs.

After a breakfast of break and milk the young woman tidied and cleaned the two small rooms. She then began to make bread. Whilst kneading the bread she went outside to see what the day was like. She felt the cool air on her face and arms because clouds were still hiding the heat and light from the sun. She knew the heat of the day would slowly appear after two hours and after that, three people would arrive to collect loaves of bread for their day.

After the three people had collected their loaves the young woman went around to the back of the house where the woman was sitting the day before.

The woman was sitting still with her eyes closed as the young woman came and sat opposite her.

She saw once again that the woman's face looked more serene than when she had first met her. The young woman had a sense that the calmness and peace in the woman's face was very pure. Again, she could only liken her serene state to the innocence of a flower or the face of a child.

Sitting down opposite her and looking at her, she noticed her thoughts slowed down so much that there was only the occasional thought. She was sitting being still with this woman and not thinking as much as usual.

Several times she would suddenly be aware that she had been in state she could not describe but which was very pleasant. It was neither sleep nor being in a trance, but it was so relaxed she wanted more of it. She felt she didn't want the woman to open her eyes. She felt she didn't want her to leave and go on her journey more south. She too closed her eyes.

Some time after she opened her eyes, she saw the woman also open her eyes and was not at all surprised to see the young woman sitting opposite her. Even after some time the woman did not speak.

The sun was setting and they got up to go inside the dwelling. When the sun had set the young woman began to make the second batch of bread. Whilst kneading the bread she went outside to see what the day was like. She felt the warm air on her face and arms because of the heat still rising from the hot earth. She knew the cooler night air would slowly appear after two hours and after that, three people would arrive to collect loaves of bread for the next day.

When they had gone the woman sat with her as they ate the bread she had made along with the vegetables and milk she had exchanged for loaves of bread. As the fire died down they fell asleep in their beds.

*

The young woman woke and saw the poor light of the pre-dawn darkness. She turned and acknowledged the light again then she slipped out of bed.

She bathed then dressed and went to revive the embers of the fire from the previous night's cooking. She added small dry twigs, then small branches then laid three logs on the smoking logs.

After a breakfast of break and milk the young woman tidied and cleaned the two small rooms. She then began to make bread. Whilst kneading the bread she went outside to see what the day was like. She felt the cool air on her face and arms because clouds were still hiding the heat and light from the sun. She knew the heat of the day would slowly appear after two hours and after that, three people would arrive to collect loaves of bread for their day.

After the three people had collected their loaves the young woman went around to the back of the house where the woman was sitting the day before.

The woman was sitting still with her eyes closed as the young woman came and sat opposite her.

She saw once again that the woman's face looked more serene than when she had first met her. The young woman had a sense that the calmness and peace in the woman's face was very pure. Again, she could only liken her serene state to the innocence of a flower or the face of a child.

Sitting down opposite her and looking at her, she noticed her thoughts slowed down so much that there was only the occasional thought. She was sitting being still with this woman and not thinking as much as usual. Several times she would suddenly be aware that she had been in state she could not describe but which was very pleasant. It was neither sleep nor being in a trance, but it was so relaxed she wanted more of it. She felt she didn't want the woman to open her eyes. She felt she didn't want her to leave and go on her journey more south. She too closed her eyes.

Some time after she opened her eyes, she saw the woman was not there. She continued to sit in stillness with her eyes closed.

The sun was setting and she got up to go inside the dwelling. When the sun had set the young woman began to make the second batch of bread. Whilst kneading the bread she went outside to see what the day was like. She felt the warm air on her face and arms because of the heat still rising from the hot earth. She knew the cooler night air would slowly appear after two hours and after that, three people would arrive to collect loaves of bread for the next day.

When they had gone, the young woman sat and ate the bread she had made along with the vegetables and milk she had exchanged for loaves of bread. As the fire died down she fell asleep in her bed.

*

The young woman woke and saw the poor light of the pre-dawn darkness. She turned and acknowledged the light again then she slipped out of bed.

She bathed then dressed and went to revive the embers of the fire from the previous night's cooking. She added small dry twigs, then small branches then laid three logs on the smoking logs.

After a breakfast of break and milk the young woman tidied and cleaned the two small rooms. She then began to make bread. Whilst kneading the bread she went outside to see what the day was like. She felt the cool air on her face and arms because clouds were still hiding the heat and light from the sun. She knew the heat of the day would slowly appear after two hours and after that, three people would arrive to collect loaves of bread for their day.

After the three people had collected their loaves the young woman went around to the back of the house where the woman had sat the day before.

Sitting down she noticed her thoughts slowed down so much that she was aware there were no more thoughts. She was sitting being still. She was conscious of her happiness but she could not see that it radiated from her eyes like a beacon.

Some time after she opened her eyes. She saw a young woman. The young woman had brought her bread. She continued to sit in stillness with her eyes closed.

✳

The woman woke and saw the poor light of the pre-dawn darkness. She turned and acknowledged the light again then she slipped out of bed.

She bathed then dressed and went outside to the back of the dwelling and sat on a log in the cool morning.

She felt the presence of the woman who had sat there with her for many days. Her presence was stronger, as if they were the same consciousness.

Sitting down she noticed her thoughts had slowed down so much that she was aware there were no more thoughts. She was sitting being still.

Later when she opened her eyes she saw some young women were sitting around her. She saw their yearning for the happiness she had discovered inside.

They had brought her bread, milk and vegetables. She closed her eyes and continued to sit in stillness.

The Teacher

Like Groundhog Day, it can seem that repeated effort keeps on returning us to the same place. But with perseverance, eventually we see who we are and we are released.

The boy was tired but kept on walking until mid- morning. He realised that he was tired because he had been walking so much, so he stopped for some refreshment and to rest.

He found a place to drink some water. It had a bench behind a table facing the road, which was steaming from the hot sun.

Some time after he sat down, he noticed a man on the other end of the long wooden bench. He was wearing baggy khaki trousers and a khaki shirt.

The man smiled and nodded at the boy sitting on the other end of the bench.

As he smiled, a single tear ran from the corner of each eye down each cheek, which he quickly wiped.

The boy noticed how happy this stranger seemed, even though he was old and on his own. He wondered for a while how anyone could be so happy.

When the man smiled at the boy and nodded, the boy noticed him wiping a tear from either eye. The boy could see these were tears of happiness.

There was no conversation as neither talked. The boy's head was full of concerns about his future. His eyes looked this way and then the other way. He was a little fidgety and not particularly calm. He was not concerned with the old man.

As he thought about the next part of his walking, he realised how tired he was. He was worried he would never find a home and this made him worry that he would never be happy.

The old man was calm and sat quite still as he looked out from the table onto the road outside. His mind was free of thoughts as he stared straight ahead. He was not concerned about the future. He was not concerned about anything. He was minding his own business and detached from everything in the outside world. He was as happy as he could be as he sat smiling, looking straight ahead onto the road outside.

Again the boy noticed how happy this stranger seemed, even though he was old and on his own. He wondered for a while how anyone could be so happy.

After some time, the man felt rested and straightened his skinny legs, rose from the bench and left. The boy sat looking ahead at the road for some time. He finished his cool drink and realised it was mid-morning. He thought he should get walking on the hot dusty road again to make progress.

*

After two hours of walking, the heat from the bright hot midday sun forced the boy to find more water. He saw a similar sheltered building in the distance and quickened his pace in anticipation of quenching his thirst.

Like the previous building, it was dark but he found a long wooden bench behind a table facing the road and sat down. As his eyes adjusted from the bright sunlight to the unlit coolness of the building, he saw that the man from his previous stop had got there before him and was sitting on the end of his bench.

There was no conversation as neither talked. The

boy's head was still full of concerns about his future. His eyes looked this way and then the other way. He was a little fidgety and not particularly calm. He was not concerned with the old man.

As he thought about the next part of his walking, he realised how tired he was. He was worried he would never find a home and this made him worry that he would never be happy.

The old man was calm and sat quite still as he looked out from the table onto the road outside. His mind was free of thoughts as he stared straight ahead. He was not concerned about the future. He was not concerned about anything. He was minding his own business and detached from everything in the outside world. He was as happy as he could be as he sat smiling, looking straight ahead onto the road outside.

The boy noticed again how happy this stranger seemed, even though he was old and on his own. He wondered for a while how anyone could be so happy and he realised he didn't have any answers to how he could be as happy.

After some time, the man felt rested and straightened his skinny legs, rose from the bench and left. The boy sat looking ahead at the road for some time. He finished his cool drink and realised it was past midday. He thought he should begin walking on the hot dusty road again to make progress.

*

After two hours of walking, the heat from the bright hot

early afternoon sun forced the boy to find more water. He saw a similar sheltered building in the distance and quickened his pace in anticipation of quenching his thirst.

Like the previous building, it was dark but he found a long wooden bench behind a table facing the road and sat down. As his eyes adjusted from the bright sunlight to the unlit coolness of the building, once again he saw that the man from his previous stop had got there before him and was sitting on the end of his bench.

There was no conversation as neither talked. The boy's head was full of concerns about his future. His eyes looked this way and then the other way. He was a little fidgety and not particularly calm. He was not concerned with the old man. Instead, his mind turned to how tired he was. He was worried he would never find a home and this made him worry that he would never be happy.

The old man was calm and sat quite still as he looked out from the table onto the road outside. His mind was free of thoughts as he stared straight ahead. He was not concerned about the future. He was not concerned about anything. He was minding his own business and detached from everything in the outside world. He was as happy as he could be as he sat smiling, looking straight ahead onto the road outside.

The boy noticed again how happy this stranger seemed, even though he was old and on his own. He wondered for a while how anyone could be so happy and once again he realised he didn't have any answers to how he could be as happy.

But he was also curious and even though he was a little reluctant to strike up conversations with strangers, he asked the man.

'How come you seem so happy?'

'I am happy because I work hard just to be happy.' He looked at the boy then looked straight ahead. After some time, the man felt rested and straightened his skinny legs, rose from the bench and left.

The boy sat at the table for some time, looking ahead at the road. He finished his cool drink and realised it was past the middle of the afternoon. He thought he should begin walking on the hot dusty road again to make progress.

When he stood outside in the sun, he saw the man walking ahead of him, but he forgot about him. He started wondering if he would ever be that happy. He wanted that more than anything else he could think of.

*

After two hours of walking, the heat from his walking in the late afternoon sun forced him to find more water. He saw a similar sheltered building in the distance and quickened his pace in anticipation of quenching his thirst.

Like the previous building, it was dark but he found a long wooden bench behind a table facing the road and sat down. As his eyes adjusted from the bright sunlight to the unlit coolness of the building, once again he saw that the man from his previous stop had got there before him and was sitting on the end of his bench.

There was no conversation as neither talked. The boy's head was full of concerns about his future. His eyes looked this way and then the other way. He was a little fidgety and not particularly calm. He was not concerned with the old man.

As he thought about the next part of his walking, he realised how tired he was. He was worried he would never find a home and this made him worry that he would never be happy.

The old man was calm and sat quite still as he looked out from the table onto the road outside. His mind was free of thoughts as he stared straight ahead. He was not concerned about the future. He was not concerned about anything. He was minding his own business and detached from everything in the outside world. He was as happy as he could be as he sat smiling, looking straight ahead onto the road outside.

The boy noticed again how happy this stranger seemed, even though he was old and on his own. He wondered for a while how anyone could be so happy and once again he realised he didn't have any answers to how he could be as happy.

'I saw you walking in front me. How did you get here so much before me?'

'I saw you walking behind me. I knew you were already following my path. I don't mean the actual physical path you take when you are walking, even though it seems that way. You are about to follow the path in life I took.'

'How do you know that?'

'I have been where you are now going. I did it in the past and you will do it in the future. But we are both here now. Whichever way you go, you will be following me. So, I will be there with you.'

After some time, the man felt rested and straightened his skinny legs, rose from the bench and left.

The boy sat at the table looking ahead at the road for some time. He finished his cool drink and realised it was late afternoon. He thought he should begin walking on the hot dusty road again to make progress.

When he stood outside in the sun, he saw the man walking ahead of him, but he forgot about him. He started wondering if he would ever be that happy. He wanted that more than anything else he could think of. He was determined to ask the man more about this if he met him again.

*

After two hours of walking, the heat from the bright hot early morning sun forced the boy to find more water. He saw a similar sheltered building in the distance and quickened his pace in anticipation of quenching his thirst.

Like the previous building, it was dark but he found a long wooden bench behind a table facing the road and sat down. As his eyes adjusted from the bright sunlight to the unlit coolness of the building, once again he saw that the man from his previous stop had got there before him and was sitting on the end of his bench.

There was no conversation as neither talked. The boy's head was full of concerns about his future. His eyes looked this way and then the other way. He was a little fidgety and not particularly calm. He was not concerned with the old man.

As he thought about the next part of his walking,

he realised how tired he was. He was worried he would never find a home and this made him worry that he would never be happy.

The old man was calm and sat quite still as he looked out from the table onto the road outside. His mind was free of thoughts as he stared straight ahead. He was not concerned about the future. He was not concerned about anything. He was minding his own business and detached from everything in the outside world. He was as happy as he could be as he sat smiling, looking straight ahead onto the road outside.

The boy noticed again how happy this stranger seemed, even though he was old and on his own. He wondered for a while how anyone could be so happy and once again he realised he didn't have any answers to how he could be as happy.

'I know I asked you this before but how do you work hard just to be happy?'

'After finding that you can't find happiness outside.'

'I don't understand.'

'When you realise that the only real happiness is inside yourself, you have to work hard to uncover it.'

'Does it take long?

'Time does not come into it. It always takes effort.' He was smiling gently.

After some time the man felt rested and straightened his skinny legs, rose from the bench and left.

The boy sat at the table looking ahead at the road for some time. He finished his cool drink and realised it was past the middle of the morning. He thought he should begin walking on the hot dusty road again to make progress.

When he stood outside in the sun, he saw the man walking ahead of him, but he forgot about him. He started wondering if he would ever be that happy. He wanted that more than anything else he could think of. He was determined to ask the man more about this if he met him again.

*

After two hours of late morning walking, the heat from the midday sun forced him to find refreshments. He saw a sheltered building in the distance and quickened his pace in anticipation of quenching his thirst.

Like the previous buildings, it was dark but he found a long wooden bench behind a table facing the road and sat down. As his eyes adjusted from the bright sunlight to the unlit coolness of the building he could see he was on his own.

As he thought about the next part of his walking, he realised how tired he was. He was worried he would never find a home and this made him worry that he would never be happy.

Just after he started his cold drink, the old man came and sat on the other end of the long wooden bench he was sitting on.

There was no conversation as neither talked. The old man was calm and sat quite still as he looked out from the table onto the road outside. His mind was free of thoughts as he stared straight ahead. He was not concerned about the future. He was not concerned about anything. He was minding his own business and quite detached from others. He was as happy as he could be as he sat smiling, looking straight ahead onto the road outside.

The more the boy thought about how calm and happy the old man seemed, the less he wanted to pursue his questioning from the day before. Just sitting with him made him feel a little easier about himself so, he sat and felt even better about himself.

The longer he sat, the more he realised that the man sitting with him was somehow showing him how to be happy.

Eventually the old man raised himself to his feet, looked at the boy, smiled and left.

The boy sat at the table looking ahead at the road for some time. He finished his cool drink and realised it was much later than he thought. Most of the day had passed and it was now late afternoon. He thought he should begin the last walk of the day.

*

The old man was calm and sat quite still as he looked out from the table onto the road outside. His mind was free of thoughts as he stared straight ahead. He was not concerned about the future. He was not concerned about anything. He was minding his own business and detached from everything in the outside world. He was as happy as he could be as he sat smiling, looking straight ahead onto the road outside.

Once more, as the boy thought about the how calm and happy the old man seemed, the less he wanted to pursue questioning him. He realised that he felt strangely calm when he was in this man's presence. But because of this new feeling of inner calmness and especially because only yesterday he had sat with the old man for hours without talking, he felt he should mention this.

'Yesterday I felt the calmest I have ever felt. My childhood was chaotic and so there was never inner security or the feeling of calmness like I felt yesterday. I felt that the damage, the hole inside me from my childhood had somehow been filled in. What is this calmness?'

'It does not have a good enough name because words can't describe it adequately enough.' The old man was staring straight ahead into the distance. 'It is being conscious of your own inner stillness. What you were conscious of is your very nature. Your nature is not to have thoughts and to be still.'

The boy considered what the man said for some time and felt he had to ask him more whilst he was still with him.

'I was so surprised that inside there is a part of me that is so happy. How can I be in that state longer, I mean every day? How do I get to know that part of me better?'

There was silence as the man looked straight ahead. Eventually he turned to the boy, looked at him, smiled and spoke.

'If you are hungry enough for it, you will make the effort to have it. It requires effort at wanting just stillness. Some have suffered so much that healing the damage from their childhood is the most important aim of their life. As you said, it helps to heal your suffering, to fill in the hole inside you from your childhood, the hole in your soul.'

'I know deep inside me what you say is right. But how do I find out more?'

'If you pursue this, you will uncover it.' The old man raised himself to his feet and left. The boy sat at the table looking ahead at the road for some time. He finished his cool drink and realised he should carry on with the rest of the morning walk.

*

After two hours of walking, tiredness forced the boy to find refreshments. He saw a sheltered building in the distance and quickened his pace in anticipation of quenching his thirst. But inside there was nowhere to sit. There was someone in every possible seat.

'Why are you all here?' He asked an elderly man.

'We are having a meeting with a local leader.'

'Is it soon?'

'Yes, it will start in a short while.'

'Will it last long?'

'Sometimes all evening, late into the night.'

The boy waited with them for some time but he saw that he was not going to have peace and rest in a group of people, so he left and walked back onto the road.

After a short while he saw another refreshment building and was relieved to find it was empty. He found a long wooden bench behind a table facing the road and sat down.

He felt at peace away from the gossip which was all about what had been and about what might be. Away from the turmoil of competitive thinking amongst this group, he was now closer to his own self. He was calmer.

He looked out on to the road. He considered what he should be doing. He thought about what the old man had said and wondered what he should do to find happiness. The words the man had said echoed in his head, 'When you realise that the only real happiness is inside yourself, you have to work hard to uncover it. Time does not come into it.' Then he had said, 'It always takes effort. If you pursue this, you will uncover it.'

'What is the work?' the boy thought. 'How do I look inside myself? It's not like I can read about me like reading a book. He never said how to do it.'

He felt lost. He trusted this man as neither had any investment in the other. They had nothing material to gain form the other. He trusted him because when he asked him about his happiness, he did not try and sell it to him.

As he was thinking this, he saw from the dark area behind him a man moving towards the other end of the wooden bench. It was the old man in the khaki trousers and shirt.

The old man was calm and sat quite still as he looked out from the table onto the road outside. His mind seemed free of thoughts as he stared straight ahead. He didn't seem concerned about anything. He was minding his own business and quite detached from others. He didn't seem worried about anything. He appeared to be as happy as he could be as he sat smiling, looking straight ahead onto the road outside.

'I need your help. You said if I tried to uncover my

happiness, I would find it. Since we spoke, I have thought about nothing else other than this. But I don't feel I am getting any closer to being happy.' The boy noticed the old man had a gentle smile on his face as he continued to stare straight ahead for some time.

'You have seen that your happiness is inside you already. Happiness is your nature. This is one of the most important achievements anyone can make in their life. You have thought a lot about happiness but your happiness can't be uncovered by thinking about it. Thinking is the actual veil which hides it. When you can stop thinking, even for a few seconds, you will see that in the space between your last thought and the next one that comes, there is just consciousness, stillness, without any thought.'

'How do I do that?'

'You can only be it. It is achieved by ceaseless effort to be it. You have to have a hunger for happiness like there is nothing else you desire.'

'How do I make the effort?'

'Your mind needs to be controlled by you so it is not wondering off in a different direction of thought every few moments. Only when it is still, can you see what you are.'

'I don't understand. How do I do this?'

'First, mind control. Then the aim is to find out what you are by being still.'

'How do I control my mind and how can I be still?'

'Try it on your own. This needs repeated and ceaseless daily focusing the mind on this one thing. At the same time, you also have to live and eat. But giving yourself times when you are still every day is the most important thing you can do. It is vital.' His eyes looked straight ahead, then he turned to the boy, smiled and left.

*

The boy didn't begin his early morning walk as usual. Instead, he sat upright where he had slept and looked at what the old man had said. As he stared ahead, he tried to look at what he was.

'Am I my parent's son? No, I am not just that. Am I this person on a daily path of discovery? No, I am more than that.' He closed his eyes to see clearer inside. 'Ok so I am not just my parent's son, or this person on a path of discovery. I am not those. So what am I?'

After tiring himself with this question he got up to begin his walking.

As he walked he kept on asking himself the same question, 'What am I?' After some time he became so lost for ways to see himself clearly that he looked for somewhere to rest.

He was feeling disappointed he had not been able to make any progress with looking inside for happiness. He didn't want to think about it anymore, so he gave up and just stared ahead as he walked along the road.

But the question arose more than once which he could not avoid, 'What am I?' At first, there was an answer, 'I am my memories and I am my hopes for a happy future.' Then he realised that he was looking at things outside himself. He tried to look inwards but felt blocked. Next he became distracted by the conditions of where he was walking.

The day was showing signs of rain, so he thought he would look for cover in a building. After a while he came to a rest house, but in it were many people who had also sensed the drop in air pressure along with the darkening skies. It was not full and he could have taken refuge from the oncoming rain but he did not want to spend the afternoon and perhaps the night in a crowded room.

'You should stay here.' Said a middle aged man as he walked past it. 'There isn't another shelter like this for miles, except for ruined ones. There's a whole night of rain coming. It could last for days. You'll get drenched if you carry on.'

The boy put his hand up to thank him and carried on walking.

He quickened his pace at the warning of the man. Most of the refreshment houses were an hour or two hours apart but sometimes there were ones in between which had been abandoned, usually because of dilapidation.

Soon after midday had passed, he felt an occasional drop of rain on his face and head. He could see what looked like an abandoned refreshment house just ahead.

Knowing he was not going to make it there dry, he surrendered. He relaxed and welcomed the rain which he felt was about to become puddles and rivers by his feet. A few moments later, rain was streaming down his face and his shoes were full of rain water. He looked up at the sky which was dark everywhere, apart from an area ahead, far beyond where he was walking. In the midst of this torrential downpour, suddenly he felt as if he was being shown that the path ahead was positive and the right one to have taken. He smiled and walked with his arms out wide, welcoming not just the rain but whatever life was.

*

Unlike the previous refreshment buildings, it was not so dark because of a hole in the roof and there was no one there. He found a toppled over long wooden bench behind an upturned table which he straightened up. He sat on the bench facing the road. He looked around him and as he turned back to face the road, he saw the old man in khaki enter through the door and sit at the other end of the wooden bench.

The old man was calm and sat quite still as he looked out from the table onto the road outside. His mind was free of thoughts as he stared straight ahead. He was not concerned about the future. He was not concerned about anything. He was minding his own business and detached from everything in the outside world. He was as happy as he could be as he sat smiling, looking straight ahead onto the road outside.

After a long time, the man turned to look at him. They exchanged an almost identical smile as they sat in silence.

The boy broke the long silence.

'How do you not have thoughts?'

'Thoughts are seen and stopped by going inside to look inwards.'

'I tried looking today. At first I was looking outwards at what I am. Then I started looking inwards but I was blocked. I couldn't see a way inside.'

'When you are looking outside, if it is dark, you can't see, so you turn the lights on, then you can see. When you are looking inside, you can't see if it is light with distractions from outside, so you turn the outer lights off by closing your eyes. Only then you begin to see.'

The boy closed his eyes and sat still.

*

The boy woke from his sleep and immediately sat on the bench and closed his eyes. After some hours sitting on and off with his eyes closed he was aware of the faint sound of the man in khaki sitting down at the other end of the wooden bench.

The boy opened his eyes. After a long time, the man turned to look at him. They exchanged an almost identical smile as they sat in silence.

The old man was calm and sat quite still as he looked out from the table onto the road outside. His mind was free of thoughts as he stared straight ahead. He was not concerned about the future. He was not concerned about anything. He was minding his own business and detached from everything in the outside world. He was as happy as he could be as he sat smiling, looking straight ahead onto the road outside.

The boy broke the long silence.

'At first all I could see were blurred red patterns in front of my eyes. Then my eyeball stopped moving but then I noticed my thoughts were coming one after another. I couldn't stop them easily, even when I tried hard. They just surface from nowhere.'

'Each of us experiences this when we begin. But when the mind is tethered like an animal to one spot, it does not cause problems, so thoughts do not keep on appearing so easily. What is needed is mind control.

'How do I tether my thoughts so they stop appearing?

'The mind can be tethered so thoughts stop appearing so quickly. You either tether it by following your breathing or repeating a sound. A sound is easier so I will let you hear one. When thoughts appear, bring back the sound to the front of your consciousness. However, thoughts will always try and appear.'

He turned to the boy and pronounced a sound. He leant towards the boy, nodding his head he invited him with his upturned right hand to repeat the sound, which the boy did.

The man in khaki said the sound softer and also indicated by lowering his downturned hand nearer and nearer to the floor to say it lower and softer, which the boy did. The man then indicated to say the sound more quietly, which the boy again did.

Once again the man indicated that the boy should say it even quieter, which the boy did. When the boy was saying it silently but still moving his lips, the man indicated with his fingers running down over his eyes that the boy should close his eyes, which the boy did.

Some time later the boy opened his eyes and looked straight ahead into the distance. He didn't move and his breathing was still very slow. Then he closed his eyes again, silently producing the sound inside. Later he opened his eyes and looked straight ahead, then he spoke.

'I have never felt so happy. I feel at peace. I am the calmest I have ever been. After a while thoughts did come but bringing back the sound made them go.' He was radiating a smile which the old man recognised.

'This is meditation. It is this simple. It should be your first mental activity of each day and it should be repeated as often as you can do it throughout the day.' As soon as he said this he looked at the boy, smiled and walked outside as there was a break in the storm.

*

The boy woke from his sleep and immediately sat on the bench and closed his eyes. After some hours he was aware of the faint sound of the man in khaki sitting down at the other end of the wooden bench. He opened his eyes.

After a long time, the man turned to look at him. They exchanged an almost identical smile as they sat in silence.

The old man was calm and sat quite still as he looked out from the table onto the road outside. His mind was free of thoughts as he stared straight ahead. He was not concerned about the future. He was not concerned about anything. He was minding his own business and detached from everything in the outside world. He was as happy as he could be as he sat smiling, looking straight ahead onto the road outside.

The boy broke the long silence.

'I now see what you explained to me. I feel I have more control over thoughts coming and going. There's also a deep peace I can't describe. It is just peace.'

'Meditation is an activity to purify the mind so it is controlled. When it is controlled you can then begin to be more conscious of what you are. Now you know how to control your mind with meditation, you can begin to ask what you are.

'How do you find out what you are?'

'You have to know the Self in yourself by yourself. This is the highest state. Your nature is happiness. Your nature is a state of consciousness which is happiness.

Our difficulty seeing this is because it is veiled by our ignorance. We are born happy. But, we see suffering and we experience suffering. We are told that we can be made happy again by the world. But this does not work. We are told we will succeed if we work hard. But this does not work.

We are conditioned and programmed by this ignorance so much that we lose touch with our inner happiness.

We have to work hard to get back in touch with our natural consciousness, our state of inner happiness. We have to remove the darkness, the ignorance that the world wants us to believe. Knowledge leads to the path of release from suffering, ignorance to worldly pursuits of all possessions.'

'I find it difficult to understand how to do this.'

'Asking what you are is the process of removing your ignorance so that you can see your inner state of happiness.

We have to ask what we are, our whole life. That question must be at the forefront of your consciousness so that your happiness is your main priority. It is not that you have to keep on asking yourself the same question all the time, What am I? But that you constantly try and be what you are and avoid what you are not.

Hearing this is vital. Reflecting on this is more powerful. Being this is many times more powerful.'

'When is the best time to do this?'

'Now and all the time. When you sit quietly with your eyes closed and you battle your thoughts so that they go, what is left is your consciousness without thoughts, the Witness.

When at other times you are active with your eyes open, do the same. You find out what you actually are by eliminating what you are not.

As soon as he said this he looked at the boy, smiled and walked outside as there was a break in the storm.

*

The boy had been walking all morning and saw a rest house ahead of him. He slowed down to look and saw the man in khaki standing outside. The boy walked towards him and as he did so, he noticed the old man was looking at him with the gentle smile he always had when he sat with him. The man beckoned with his hand for the boy to come into the rest house.

Once inside, they sat at either end or a wooden bench behind a table. They both stared ahead at first. Then they both closed their eyes. After some hours the boy straightened himself up and looked at the old man who on hearing the rustling of the boy, also opened his eyes.

The old man was calm and sat quite still as he looked

out from the table onto the road outside. His mind was free of thoughts as he stared straight ahead. He was not concerned about the future. He was not concerned about anything. He was minding his own business and detached from everything in the outside world. He was as happy as he could be as he sat smiling, looking straight ahead onto the road outside.

'I am still not clear about what I am.' The boy said.

'Try looking for the answer by elimination. When you ask what you are, try identifying what you are not. You only find out what you actually are by eliminating what you are not. This is removing your ignorance.

You might consider your body to be you but using anything attached to the five senses to be yourself is like holding onto a crocodile's tale to cross a river. When you see what you are not, only then can you see what you are.'

*

When the man in Khaki had gone, the boy closed his eyes and followed what the man had suggested. He continued this path which he now knew was his path. He sat in stillness for hours every day.

After days in the same rest house, the boy decided to move on and walk back on the road. He had not seen the man in khaki since he told him about the crocodile's tail and he wanted his help.

He had spent much of every day looking at what he was and what he was not, both with his eyes closed and with his eyes open.

He now saw that he was at another block in finding out what he was. He felt he was not finding out about his inner self and so he went back on the road to see if he would meet up with the man.

He set off walking in the early morning warmth and by the middle of the afternoon he was sitting in the third rest house of the day.

He sat with his closed eyes using the sound the man had given him to make thoughts less frequent until there were some moments without them. During these moments he felt a deep peace.

He was brought to open his eyes by the sense that the man was sitting on the end of the wooden bench he was sitting on.

After a long time, the man turned to look at him. They exchanged an almost identical smile as they sat in silence.

The old man was calm and sat quite still as he looked out from the table onto the road outside. His mind was free of thoughts as he stared straight ahead. He was not concerned about the future. He was not concerned about anything. He was minding his own business and detached from everything in the outside world. He was as happy as he could be as he sat smiling, looking straight ahead onto the road outside.

The boy broke the long silence.

'I keep on getting distracted by all sorts of thoughts. A lot of the thoughts are to do with small fears.'

'Fear of losing what we see as being us and ours is overcome by keeping up the questioning of what we are.

Acquiring possessions such as money, things, power,

influence or knowledge to make you happy makes you unhappy because all possessions lead to fear of their use and loss. Fear and loss make us think we will be happier if we can more securely possess them, so an endless pursuit begins. Loss anxiety makes us try harder to possess what does not even make us happy. This applies to the very small as well as the big things in our life. All these things keep our thoughts going.'

*

When the man in Khaki had gone, the boy closed his eyes and followed what the man had suggested. He continued walking his path. He sat in stillness for hours every day.

After many days in the same rest house, the boy decided to move on and walk back on the road. He had not seen the man in khaki since he told him about the thoughts of small fears and now he wanted his help again.

He had spent much of every day looking at what he was and what he was not, both with his eyes closed and with his eyes open.

He now saw that he was at another block in finding out what he was. He felt he was not finding out about his inner self and so he went back on the road to see if he would meet up with the man.

He set off walking in the early morning warmth and by the middle of the afternoon he was sitting in the third rest house of the day.

He sat with closed eyes using the sound the man had given him to make thoughts less frequent until there were some moments without them. During these brief moments he felt a deep peace.

He was brought to open his eyes by the sense that the man was sitting on the end of the wooden bench, which he was.

After a long time, the man turned to look at him. They exchanged an almost identical smile as they sat in silence.

The old man was calm and sat quite still as he looked out from the table onto the road outside. His mind was free of thoughts as he stared straight ahead. He was not concerned about the future. He was not concerned about anything. He was minding his own business and detached from everything in the outside world. He was as happy as he could be as he sat smiling, looking straight ahead onto the road outside.

The boy broke the long silence.

'I am stuck again. I keep getting thoughts about the most peaceful state I can be in. I also get thoughts of the most beautiful place I could be.'

'Don't be misled by beauty because Beauty is something recognised outside, happiness is always inside. Happiness is what you desire most.

Don't be misled by beauty because beauty is derived from the senses, happiness is revealed inside.

Don't be misled by beauty because beauty is a synthesis of fine thinking, happiness is simply being in the heart with no thoughts.

Happiness is your only desire. To uncover this you need to give up all else. You have learnt how to have much more control of your mind.

When you have moments of stillness when there

are no thoughts, ask what you are. You will see you are not your thoughts. You will see you are not a bundle of thoughts. You will see you are the witness of thoughts. Being conscious of being the witness is just being.'

*

When the man in Khaki had gone, the boy closed his eyes and followed what the man had suggested. He continued walking his path. He sat in stillness for hours every day.

After many days in the same rest house, the boy decided to move on and walk back on the road. He had not seen the man in khaki since he told him about being the witness and now he wanted his help again.

He had spent much of every day looking at what he was and what he was not, both with his eyes closed and with his eyes open.

He now saw that he was at another block in finding out what he was. He felt he was not finding out about his inner self and so he went back on the road to see if he would meet up with the man.

He set off walking in the early morning warmth and by the middle of the afternoon he was sitting in the third rest house of the day.

He sat with closed eyes using the sound the man had given him to make thoughts less frequent until there were some moments without them. During these brief moments he felt a deep peace.

He was brought to open his eyes by the sense that the man was sitting on the end of the wooden bench, which he was.

After a long time, the man turned to look at him. They exchanged an almost identical smile as they sat in silence.

The old man was calm and sat quite still as he looked out from the table onto the road outside. His mind was free of thoughts as he stared straight ahead. He was not concerned about the future. He was not concerned about anything. He was minding his own business and detached from everything in the outside world. He was as happy as he could be as he sat smiling, looking straight ahead onto the road outside.

The boy broke the long silence.

'I am stuck again. I keep on getting thoughts. But they are not really about anything, just memories of the past and worry about the future.'

'You might see you as being your past memories or your future dreams. These are just thoughts and not you.

The past and future are not you. The past and future do not exist. Only your consciousness exists about you. Your consciousness can only exist in the present. Staying in the present gets rid of the past and future.

Keep on with this until you eliminate everything that you are not. Including your thoughts.'

*

When the man in Khaki had gone, the boy closed his eyes and followed what the man had suggested. He continued walking his path. He sat in stillness for hours every day.

After many days in the same rest house, the boy decided to move on and walk back on the road. He had not seen the man in khaki since he told him about staying in the present and now he wanted his help again.

He had spent much of every day looking at what he was and what he was not, both with his eyes closed and with his eyes open.

He now saw that he was at another block in finding out what he was. He felt he was not finding out about his inner self and so he went back on the road to see if he would meet up with the man.

He set off walking in the early morning warmth and by the middle of the afternoon he was sitting in the third rest house of the day.

He sat with closed eyes using the sound the man had given him to make thoughts less frequent until there were some moments without them. During these brief moments he felt a deep peace.

He was brought to open his eyes by the sense that the man was sitting on the end of the wooden bench, which he was.

After a long time, the man turned to look at him. They exchanged an almost identical smile as they sat in silence.

The old man was calm and sat quite still as he looked out from the table onto the road outside. His mind was free of thoughts as he stared straight ahead. He was not concerned about the future. He was not concerned about anything. He was minding his own business and detached from everything in the outside world. He was as happy as he could be as he sat smiling, looking straight ahead onto the road outside.

The boy broke the long silence.

'I am stuck again. I keep on getting thoughts. But they are not really about anything.'

'We need to restrain our mind. Giving up all desires except uncovering what you are, which is your happiness, includes restraining the mind by restraining speaking and action. Stopping these activities leads to Self Knowledge. So solitude is your friend.

To have solitude you don't have to be alone, you just have to be detached from the world. To restrain your speech doesn't mean you can't speak, just that you are not inclined to. To restrain actions doesn't mean you can't do things, it is just that you are not inclined to because you want to stay with your inner happiness.'

*

When the man in Khaki had gone, the boy closed his eyes and followed what the man had suggested. He continued walking his path. He sat in stillness for hours every day.

After many days in the same rest house, the boy decided to move on and walk back on the road. He had not seen the man in khaki since he told him about staying in the present and now he wanted his help again.

He had spent much of every day looking at what he was and what he was not, both with his eyes closed and with his eyes open.

He now saw that he was at another block in finding out what he was. He felt he was not finding out about his inner self and so he went back on the road to see if he would meet up with the man.

He set off walking in the early morning warmth and

by the middle of the afternoon he was sitting in the third rest house of the day.

He sat with closed eyes using the sound the man had given him to make thoughts less frequent until there were some moments without them. During these brief moments he felt a deep peace.

He was brought to open his eyes by the sense that the man was sitting on the end of the wooden bench, which he was.

After a long time, the man turned to look at him. They exchanged an almost identical smile as they sat in silence.

The old man was calm and sat quite still as he looked out from the table onto the road outside. His mind was free of thoughts as he stared straight ahead. He was not concerned about the future. He was not concerned about anything. He was minding his own business and detached from everything in the outside world. He was as happy as he could be as he sat smiling, looking straight ahead onto the road outside.

The boy broke the long silence.

'I am still getting thoughts. But again, they are not really about anything. They disturb the calmness I have found.'

'The calmness we find inside is stillness. It is our stillness. It is our very self.

It is not possible to use words to describe it because everything about it is beyond words because it is our consciousness.

When you look at a great mountain, one of the most impressive things about it is not its size. The most impressive thing about a great mountain is not its height. What affects us the most is its stillness.

When you look at the stars in the sky, you see it is us who are moving. They are still. Stillness is your nature too and that is what your calmness is.'

*

When the man in Khaki had gone, the boy closed his eyes and followed what the man had suggested. He continued walking his path. He sat in stillness for hours every day.

After many days in the same rest house, the boy decided to move on and walk back on the road. He had not seen the man in khaki since he told him about restraining the mind and now he wanted his help again.

He had spent much of every day looking at what he was and what he was not, both with his eyes closed and with his eyes open.

He now saw that he was at another block in finding out what he was. He felt he was not finding out about his inner self and so he went back on the road to see if he would meet up with the man.

He set off walking in the early morning warmth and by the middle of the afternoon he was sitting in the third rest house of the day.

He sat with closed eyes using the sound the man had given him to make thoughts less frequent until there were some moments without them. During these brief moments he felt a deep peace.

He was brought to open his eyes by the sense that the man was sitting on the end of the wooden bench, which he was.

After a long time, the man turned to look at him. They exchanged an almost identical smile as they sat in silence.

The old man was calm and sat quite still as he looked out from the table onto the road outside. His mind was free of thoughts as he stared straight ahead. He was not concerned about the future. He was not concerned about anything. He was minding his own business and detached from everything in the outside world. He was as happy as he could be as he sat smiling, looking straight ahead onto the road outside.

The boy broke the long silence.

'I want to know more about consciousness.'

'The ancients used to say different things about it such as, I am That, or That thou art or Be still and know that I am God.

Essentially All is one, All is one self and One is all.

Unfortunately, the scriptures broadcast this out to everyone in the hope that people will just believe it. Of course it is possible to blindly believe, but it is not knowing. Knowing can only be achieved by finding out for yourself, by yourself. All and self are no different. One is All.

*

When the man in Khaki had gone, the boy closed his eyes and followed what the man had suggested. He continued walking his path. He sat in stillness for hours every day.

After many days in the same rest house, the boy

decided to move on and walk back on the road. He had not seen the man in khaki since he told him about consciousness and one is all. He wanted his help again.

He had spent much of every day looking at what he was and what he was not, both with his eyes closed and with his eyes open.

He now saw that he was at another block in finding out what he was. He felt he was not finding out about his inner self and so he went back on the road to see if he would meet up with the man.

He set off walking in the early morning warmth and by the middle of the afternoon he was sitting in the third rest house of the day.

He sat with closed eyes using the sound the man had given him to make thoughts less frequent until there were some moments without them. During these brief moments he felt a deep peace.

He was brought to open his eyes by the sense that the man was sitting on the end of the wooden bench, which he was.

After a long time, the man turned to look at him. They exchanged an almost identical smile as they sat in silence.

The old man was calm and sat quite still as he looked out from the table onto the road outside. His mind was free of thoughts as he stared straight ahead. He was not concerned about the future. He was not concerned about anything. He was minding his own business and detached from everything in the outside world. He was as happy as he could be as he sat smiling, looking straight ahead onto the road outside.

The boy broke the long silence.

'I want to know more about what you said about consciousness and One is All.'

'Consciousness is realising that we are one with everything in the Universe. We see we are what we conjure up inside our self as God and we see that we are no different from God. The consciousness of what we see as 'I am' is what we are. Eventually we see that All is one and All is one self. All and self are no different.

Being conscious of this all the time is freedom from suffering and is happiness.

We are not suffering. We are not decay and death. We are this consciousness. We are this consciousness of stillness which is happiness.

To have seen this, you will have to have meditated until the world of individuals appears as a dream. You see you and you see all is one.

To be your self, all you need to know and be is the 'that' of 'Thou art that.'

*

When the man in Khaki had gone, the boy closed his eyes and followed what the man had suggested. He continued walking his path. He sat in stillness for hours every day.

After many days in the same rest house, the boy decided to move on and walk back on the road. He had not seen the man in khaki since he told him about consciousness and seeing the dream. He wanted his help again.

He had spent much of every day looking at what he

was and what he was not, both with his eyes closed and with his eyes open.

He now saw that he was at another block in finding out what he was. He felt he was not finding out about his inner self and so he went back on the road to see if he would meet up with the man.

He set off walking in the early morning warmth and by the middle of the afternoon he was sitting in the third rest house of the day.

He sat with closed eyes using the sound the man had given him to make thoughts less frequent until there were some moments without them. During these brief moments he felt a deep peace.

He was brought to open his eyes by the sense that the man was sitting on the end of the wooden bench, which he was.

After a long time, the man turned to look at him. They exchanged an almost identical smile as they sat in silence.

The old man was calm and sat quite still as he looked out from the table onto the road outside. His mind was free of thoughts as he stared straight ahead. He was not concerned about the future. He was not concerned about anything. He was minding his own business and detached from everything in the outside world. He was as happy as he could be as he sat smiling, looking straight ahead onto the road outside.

The boy broke the long silence.

'I want to know more about meditation and consciousness.'

'Meditation brings you to one pointedness of your

consciousness. You see there is no division between consciousness in meditation and consciousness when your eyes are open.

The world of individuals appears as a dream. You see all is one. You see there is no division. You are that. We are only distracted by our thoughts.

You see that you are the witness. This consciousness becomes the lens through which you see everything.

Giving up the world as we have seen it, giving up thoughts, giving up the body as we have seen it and giving up all scriptures lets us see and know 'all is one self,' so we can just be it.'

*

When the man in Khaki had gone, the boy closed his eyes and followed what the man had suggested. He continued walking his path. He sat in stillness for hours every day.

After many days in the same rest house, the boy decided to move on and walk back on the road. He had not seen the man in khaki since he told him about consciousness and seeing the dream. He wanted his help again.

He had spent much of every day looking at what he was and what he was not, both with his eyes closed and with his eyes open.

He now saw that he was at another block in finding out what he was. He felt he was not finding out about his inner self and so he went back on the road to see if he would meet up with the man.

He set off walking in the early morning warmth and

by the middle of the afternoon he was sitting in the third rest house of the day.

He sat with closed eyes using the sound the man had given him to make thoughts less frequent until there were some moments without them. During these brief moments he felt a deep peace.

He was brought to open his eyes by the sense that the man was sitting on the end of the wooden bench, which he was.

After a long time, the man turned to look at him. They exchanged an almost identical smile as they sat in silence.

The old man was calm and sat quite still as he looked out from the table onto the road outside. His mind was free of thoughts as he stared straight ahead. He was not concerned about the future. He was not concerned about anything. He was minding his own business and detached from everything in the outside world. He was as happy as he could be as he sat smiling, looking straight ahead onto the road outside.

The boy broke the long silence.

'I want to know more about being still.'

'Always remember that giving up the world as we have seen it, giving up thoughts, giving up the body as we have seen it and giving up all scriptures lets us see and know all is one self, so we can just be it.'

'How do I know when I have done this?'

'There is no such thing as having done it because that is in the past. You have to always be doing it.

But since you ask, perfection is when we don't see our Self as the body. Perfection is when we don't look for any enjoyment outside. Perfection is when our thoughts don't turn outside.' When he said this he looked at the boy, smiled, slowly raised himself up and left.

*

When the man in Khaki had gone, the boy closed his eyes and followed what the man had suggested. He continued walking his path. He sat in stillness for hours every day.

After many days in the same rest house, the boy decided to move on and walk back on the road. He had not seen the man in khaki since he told him about consciousness and one is all and all is one. He wanted his help again.

He had spent much of every day looking at what he was and what he was not, both with his eyes closed and with his eyes open.

He now saw that he was at another block in finding out what he was. He felt he was not finding out about his inner self and so he went back on the road to see if he would meet up with the man.

He set off walking in the early morning warmth and by the middle of the afternoon he was sitting in the third rest house of the day.

He sat with closed eyes using the sound the man had given him to make thoughts less frequent until there were some moments without them. During these brief moments he felt a deep peace.

He was brought to open his eyes by the sense that the man was sitting on the end of the wooden bench, which he was.

145

After a long time, the man turned to look at him. They exchanged an almost identical smile as they sat in silence.

The old man was calm and sat quite still as he looked out from the table onto the road outside. His mind was free of thoughts as he stared straight ahead. He was not concerned about the future. He was not concerned about anything. He was minding his own business and detached from everything in the outside world. He was as happy as he could be as he sat smiling, looking straight ahead onto the road outside.

The boy broke the long silence.

'I want to know more about giving up what is outside and what is inside.'

Giving up the world as we have seen it, giving up thoughts as we saw them, giving up the body as we have seen it and giving up all scriptures lets us see and know 'all is one self,' so we can just be it.

But it is not giving up anything at all. Nothing is lost. Nothing is gained. It is simply uncovering what we can't see about it. It is removing our ignorance about it. It is removing the darkness in us by lighting up what is there and seeing what we are. It is not adding something or removing something. It is simply seeing what is here.

＊

When the man in Khaki had gone, the boy closed his eyes and followed what the man had suggested. He continued walking his path. He sat in stillness for hours every day.

After many days in the same rest house, the boy

decided to move on and walk back on the road. He had not seen the man in khaki since he told him about consciousness and one is all and all is one. He wanted his help again.

He had spent much of every day looking at what he was and what he was not, both with his eyes closed and with his eyes open.

He now saw that he was at another block in finding out what he was. He felt he was not finding out about his inner self and so he went back on the road to see if he would meet up with the man.

He set off walking in the early morning warmth and by the middle of the afternoon he was sitting in the third rest house of the day.

He sat with closed eyes using the sound the man had given him to make thoughts less frequent until there were some moments without them. During these brief moments he felt a deep peace.

He was brought to open his eyes by the sense that the man was sitting on the end of the wooden bench, which he was.

After a long time, the man turned to look at him. They exchanged an almost identical smile as they sat in silence.

The old man was calm and sat quite still as he looked out from the table onto the road outside. His mind was free of thoughts as he stared straight ahead. He was not concerned about the future. He was not concerned about anything. He was minding his own business and detached from everything in the outside world. He was as happy as he could be as he sat smiling, looking straight ahead onto the road outside.

The boy broke the long silence.

'How are you at peace with everything?'

'When we remove our ignorance, we see how nature works. We also see that we if we accept what is in front of us without wanting to change it, we set up less resistance.

If we do everything without trying so hard. If we do everything without wanting results, progress happens more easily and more naturally.

✳

When the man in Khaki had gone, the boy closed his eyes and followed what the man had suggested. He continued walking his path. He sat in stillness for hours every day.

After many days in the same rest house, the boy decided to move on and walk back on the road. He had not seen the man in khaki since he told him about giving up struggling. He wondered when he would see him again.

He had spent much of every day looking at what he was and what he was not, both with his eyes closed and with his eyes open.

He now saw that he was at another block in finding out what he was. He felt he was not finding out about his inner self and so he went back on the road to see if he would meet up with the man.

He set off walking in the early morning warmth and by the middle of the afternoon he was sitting in the third rest house of the day.

He sat with closed eyes using the sound the man had given him to make thoughts less frequent until there were some moments without them. During these moments he felt a deep peace . . .

. . . The boy's deep peace was slowly brought to a close by the sense that someone was sitting on the end of the wooden bench, which he was sitting on. They looked familiar. As he turned to look at the person, he looked at his own arms and noticed that the hairs were all grey. His skin was wrinkled and he was wearing baggy khaki trousers and a khaki shirt. He smiled and nodded at the boy sitting on the other end of the bench.

A single tear ran from the corner of each eye down each cheek, which he quickly wiped. He saw that he was no longer a boy.

The young boy noticed how happy this stranger seemed, even though he was old and on his own. He wondered for a while how anyone could be so happy.

When the man smiled at the boy and nodded, the boy noticed him wiping a tear from either eye.

There was no conversation as neither talked. The boy's head was full of concerns about his future. His eyes looked this way and then the other way. He was a little fidgety and not particularly calm. He was not concerned with the old man.

As the young boy thought about the next part of his walking, he realised how tired he was. He was worried he would never find a home and this made him worry that he would never be happy.

The old man was calm and sat quite still as he looked out from the table onto the road outside. His mind was free of thoughts as he stared straight ahead. He was not concerned about the future. He was not concerned about anything. He was minding his own business and detached from everything. He was as happy as he could be as he sat smiling, looking straight ahead onto the road outside.

*

After two hours of walking, the heat from the bright hot midday sun forced the boy to find more water. He saw a similar sheltered building in the distance and quickened his pace in anticipation of quenching his thirst.

Like the previous building, it was dark but he found a long wooden bench behind a table facing the road and sat down. As his eyes adjusted from the bright sunlight to the unlit coolness of the building, he saw that the man from his previous stop had got there before him and was sitting on the end of his bench.

There was no conversation as neither talked. The boy's head was full of concerns about his future. His eyes looked this way and then the other way. He was a little fidgety and not particularly calm. He was not concerned with the old man.

As he thought about the next part of his walking, he realised how tired he was. He was worried he would never find a home and this made him worry that he would never be happy.

The old man was calm and sat quite still as he looked

out from the table onto the road outside. His mind was free of thoughts as he stared straight ahead. He was not concerned about the future. He was not concerned about anything. He was minding his own business and detached from everything in the outside world. He was as happy as he could be as he sat smiling, looking straight ahead onto the road outside.

The boy noticed again how happy this stranger seemed, even though he was old and on his own. He wondered for a while how anyone could be so happy and he realised he didn't have any answers to how he could be as happy.

After some time the man felt rested and straightened his skinny legs, rose from the bench and left. The boy sat looking ahead at the road for some time. He finished his cool drink and realised it was past midday. He thought he should begin walking on the hot dusty road again to make progress.

*

After two hours of walking, the heat from the bright hot early afternoon sun forced the boy to find more water. He saw a similar sheltered building in the distance and quickened his pace in anticipation of quenching his thirst.

Like the previous building it was dark but he found a long wooden bench behind a table facing the road and sat down. As his eyes adjusted from the bright sunlight to the unlit coolness of the building, once again he saw that the man from his previous stop had got there before him and was sitting on the end of his bench.

There was no conversation as neither talked. The boy's head was full of concerns about his future. His eyes looked this way and then the other way. He was a little fidgety and not particularly calm. He was not concerned with the old man.

As he thought about the next part of his walking, he realised how tired he was. He was worried he would never find a home and this made him worry that he would never be happy.

The old man was calm and sat quite still as he looked out from the table onto the road outside. His mind was free of thoughts as he stared straight ahead. He was not concerned about the future. He was not concerned about anything. He was minding his own business and detached from everything in the outside world. He was as happy as he could be as he sat smiling, looking straight ahead onto the road outside.

The boy noticed again how happy this stranger seemed, even though he was old and on his own. He wondered for a while how anyone could be so happy and once again he realised he didn't have any answers to how he could be as happy.

But he was also curious and even though he was a little reluctant to strike up conversations with strangers, he asked the man.

'How come you seem so happy?'

'I am happy because I work hard just to be happy.' He looked at the boy then looked straight ahead. After some time the man felt rested and straightened his skinny legs, rose from the bench and left.

The boy started wondering if he would ever be that

happy. He wanted that more than anything else he could think of.

*

After two hours of walking, the heat from the bright hot late afternoon sun forced him to find more water. He saw a similar sheltered building in the distance and quickened his pace in anticipation of quenching his thirst.

Like the previous building, it was dark but he found a long wooden bench behind a table facing the road and sat down. As his eyes adjusted from the bright sunlight to the unlit coolness of the building, once again he saw that the man from his previous stop had got there before him and was sitting on the end of his bench.

There was no conversation as neither talked. The boy's head was full of concerns about his future. His eyes looked this way and then the other way. He was a little fidgety and not particularly calm. He was not concerned with the old man.

As he thought about the next part of his walking, he realised how tired he was. He was worried he would never find a home and this made him worry that he would never be happy.

The old man was calm and sat quite still as he looked out from the table onto the road outside. His mind was free of thoughts as he stared straight ahead. He was not concerned about the future. He was not concerned about anything. He was minding his own business and detached from everything in the outside world. He was as happy as he could be as he sat smiling, looking straight ahead onto the road outside.

The boy noticed again how happy this stranger seemed, even though he was old and on his own. He wondered for a while how anyone could be so happy and once again he realised he didn't have any answers to how he could be as happy.

'I saw you walking in front me. How did you get here so much before me?'

'I saw you walking behind me. I knew you were already following my path. I don't mean the actual physical path you take when you are walking, even though it seems that way. You are about to follow the path in life I took.'

'How do you know that?'

'I have been where you are now going. I did it in the past and you will do it in the future. But we are both here now. Whichever way you go, you will be following me. So, I will be there with you.'

Epilogue

It's four twenty in the morning and I've woken two hours before I wanted to. I lie here and I don't move. I know I won't be able to sleep any more. But I don't move. I wait and watch my thoughts rising, churning, keeping my consciousness occupied. I know this will continue if I don't do something to stop my thoughts.

I get up out of bed and go and sit in a chair. I light some incense to remind me that I am doing something which is subtle and nothing to do with thoughts. I look at the clock to see what time I start.

I ask Why am I here? I ask How can I find happiness? I ask What am I ? I ask Who am I? Each answer is clear now but it wasn't before. So what happened to me to let me see this?

I focus on just consciousness. I focus just on the witness of consciousness. I am focusing on just being the consciousness which I use the words 'I am' for. The words 'I am' are the only way, the only words I can use to communicate this to you.

This consciousness of 'I am' is the only thing I know I really am. My past has less light and dark than a shadow because it has gone. The future does not exist. The only consciousness I have is of right now. Any attempt to be anything else is a thought about consciousness, and not consciousness itself.

All I focus on is my own consciousness as it's the only thing I know is real. It is not thinking. This simple sense of consciousness of 'I am' is the only thing I know is definitely me. It has given me happiness where there was none. It is what I see and respect in you when I see you. It is also what I see when my eyes are open and when they are closed. How did this happen?

*

I remember a fire and I remember being engulfed in it when I was just over two years old. It had happened on December 24th when there had been an accident in my parent's house. When I left hospital about six weeks later, I had woken up. This sense of being awake and conscious very slowly became clearer and clearer until I was about twelve.

At twelve, the sudden disappearance of my fourteen year old brother created a catastrophic family crisis which increased over one and a half years. My parents were distraught and I received no support from school. However, because of the stress at home, I was made exempt from caning for my errors.

With no support outside there was only one place to look. Inside. I read books and one in particular by Saint Thérèse of Lisieux touched my heart deeply. I was moved by her simplicity, gentleness, surrender and love for her God.

I took her on as my reference point, my friend, who was also a saint. I also took her as someone I could speak to and who would listen to me unconditionally. I had internalised her as an ideal person as if she were not just a religious saint but more, perhaps even as an early Guru who had attained happiness, perfection whilst alive and who knew the answer to suffering. This was successful because it helped me cope and worked for a few months. Then she faded away. What I had actively imagined her to be for me, helped me through an extremely difficult period of my childhood.

What she had done was be an example of simplicity, gentleness. She was also an example of complete surrender and unconditional love.

*

At sixteen whilst I was on a school trip to the Hayward Gallery in London, I noticed an Indian friend of mine sitting very relaxed and still with his eyes closed. He looked like he was in a state which I had never seen before. What opened my eyes was that he was in a state of happiness and peace, and so I asked him what he was doing. He said he was meditating and had learnt it from a local teacher.

Within a week I had paid my instructor with money borrowed from my parents and was using a sound to bring my distracted mind back constantly to one thing, just the sound. It was my first experience of mind control.

This mantra or japa meditation is simple inner repetition of a sound and is found in most eastern religions such as Hinduism, Jainism, Sikhism, Buddhism, and Shintoism.

I have had a varying relationship with mantra/japa meditation. It has come and gone as something I do. I occasionally use a sound to tether my mind, especially if I am finding it difficult to focus and settle my mind or be calm during meditation.

Some people do mantra/japa meditation only and find that this is what they are happy with. But one size does not suit all and I was a misfit. I found the explanation of how this type of meditation worked too simple because it lacked more in-depth explanation. There was no adequate traceable history of its origins which troubled me. There was also something uncomfortable about paying for it.

However, I didn't abandon what I saw in principle was a good thing. I didn't follow this path of meditation but used it as and when I found it necessary.

*

Instead of continuing with the mantra/japa meditation, I stopped and began reading about people who were regarded as experts who taught meditation. At first no one grabbed my attention. I read about gurus but this was the 1970s and 1980s when gurus had a questionable reputation.

One afternoon I was in conversation with two young men, who were two years older than me, who had visited a mountain in South India. They spoke of people going on pilgrimages there and of a Silent Guru who had lived there, who had died in 1950. When I asked what he taught, the answer seemed vague to me. It seemed he didn't say much but sat in silence nearly all the time. He taught through silence. A written record of over four years, showed he didn't speak on sixty percent of the days. When he did speak it was only about a hundred and fifty words.

For some unknown reason, or perhaps lack of reasoning, this interested me. I didn't understand this and so I was intrigued. How could someone who didn't say anything teach meditation?

When I started reading about him, I discovered that he didn't make any claim to teach meditation. This intrigued me even more and I needed to find an explanation for this myself. I also noticed that I heard his name mentioned more often than I had previously done.

*

A few months later, I visited the mountain in South India where this Silent Guru lived most of his life. My first visit was not just an introduction to the place and the people, it raised the question, 'What are all these people doing here around this mountain?' Some said they were only there because the mountain attracted them. Some said they were devotees of one guru or another, but most said they were there only because of the Silent Guru.

I couldn't work it out. I was also distracted by the smells, the colours, the food, the people and the hustle and bustle of India. I found it difficult to focus my mind on one thing. I couldn't even meditate there.

When I visited, I initially saw what looked and felt to me like a mausoleum. There was a large structure built over the Silent Guru's tomb. There was a dining space, an office and some basic rooms to stay in. This was where he had lived and taught by sitting in silence for decades.

What I saw with my eyes was an old graveyard converted into an ashram. Since the Silent Guru's death

160

it now seemed to me like a mausoleum. However, my intuition told me that there was something here but I just couldn't see it. There was a simple reason for this. I was looking at the wrong landscape, the landscape of the outer world. I couldn't see the inner land inside me because I didn't know how to look inside.

Because I didn't understand this, and knew I didn't, I said goodbye to the place and returned to England exhausted.

*

A year later, I was back, even though I was unable to say why.

Nothing I read seemed to give me an understanding of the Silent Guru. I couldn't come up with words to explain this place, the mountain of the Silent Guru. I walked around the mountain. I spoke to people who lived there.

I left feeling something was beginning to happen to me, but I wasn't t sure what. I couldn't put any words to it. It was intangible, subtle and there was no questioning of what it was. I knew something in me was unfolding. It seemed to me that whatever was happening inside me, there was nothing I could do to find out about it, change it or speed it up.

My outer life carried on as did whatever was happening inside me. I had given up trying to control what was happening inside me. Instead I listened.

Another year passed and I still didn't know why I was back at the foot of this mountain living in a simple rented room. Once again, I sensed that something was happening inside me but I still couldn't work it out.

To me, in photographs, the Silent Guru had a compassionate face. It seemed as if he could see me. I thought maybe I was trying to see in me what he seemed to be able to see in me. His photograph was slowly turning me inwards. I had started looking in a different direction. Turning inwards made me feel strangely good and more detached from people and the world outside. Was it really his compassionate look in his photograph that was turning me inwards? If it was, then it was so subtle. If it was, then no words were involved. If it was, then words still can't describe how it works.

I wasn't able to articulate this because I was trusting something inside me more than I was trusting things I could talk about.

What was this Silent Guru's compassionate look about? Was it just compassion? Was it that his eyes seemed as if they could see deep inside me? Was it a look of understanding? Was it a look of peace and tranquillity? I knew it wasn't only one of these. There was a look I understood inside me but could not name, no matter how much I tried.

I sensed something about him in me because somehow something was being uncovered inside me. I was identifying with something in him from his photograph. I have looked at many photographs and there is one which when I first saw it on the back of a book, sent a shiver up my spine as if this person was actually looking not just at me but deep inside me. When I look at this photograph, and I did yesterday, I see an almost questioning look and also a reassuring look. It is as if he is saying in his silence, 'You know you are you doing this because this is the right thing for you to be doing?'

*

There was no moment I can pinpoint but slowly I became conscious that there was something about the sight of the mountain which had an effect on me. I had a sense of calmness in me which I could identify with the mountain. Again, just like the Silent Guru's silence I could not put it into words. I began to understand that the silence of the guru, the effect of the mountain and what was happening in me, were all beyond words.

From what I read about the Silent Guru, I understood that most of the time he was silent. It took me some time to really understand what this silence was, what it reflected. His silence was not about not speaking. His silence was not about him not producing a sound and being quiet. His silence came from him having no thoughts. He had control over his mind so that thoughts didn't keep relentlessly appearing in his mind. This was because he was focused entirely on consciousness itself. He was able to be just consciousness. His silence was inner silence. It was about the silence of not having thoughts.

The state of having no thoughts is having a still mind. A still mind can be achieved by mantra meditation, which is what I had experienced for short periods when I did mantra/japa meditation.

The Silent Guru said that the method in his teaching was, 'Be Still' and that the truth was summed up in, 'I am that I am.'

For a long time, I didn't understand the relevance of the mountain and especially what it meant to the Silent Guru. He always maintained that the mountain was his guru and the mountain was also god. He went further and said that your Self, the Guru, the Mountain and God were all the same.

I couldn't understand this. How could they possibly all be the same? I felt lacking in perception of what was going on.

Eventually I understood the importance of the mountain to the Silent Guru. It is still. Its stillness reflects our inner stillness, the stillness of having no thoughts. To the Silent Guru, his own silence and stillness were the same at the stillness of the mountain. I hadn't seen this when I visited the mountain during my early visits. Perhaps this is what had been pulling me back to the mountain.

The Silent Guru repeatedly said that to know 'the Self' and have happiness we should ask who we are. He suggested asking the question, 'Who am I?'

He quoted the Biblical statement of 'I am that I AM.' When Moses asked God for his name he answered, 'I Am that I Am. Thus shalt you say unto the children of Israel, I Am has sent me to you.' Jehovah means I am. So, knowing the self, God is known as they are taken to be the same.

The truth of this resonated with other Biblical sayings such as 'Be still and know that I am God.' (Psalm 46) 'The kingdom of God is within you.' (Luke 17:20-21)

The Silent Guru was showing how to see the self and

how to see that it is also the supreme cosmic spirit. It doesn't matter what it is called, God or Brahman because most importantly the Silent Guru was showing how to be still, how to be the Self.

He said that if the mind becomes absorbed in the heart, by being the consciousness of 'I am,' the ego vanishes and only consciousness of the Self remains. This is what he called silence.

With constant being the consciousness of 'I am,' the consciousness of 'I am' becomes the default consciousness.

All I can tell you is I learnt this from the Silent Guru. I can't explain what he taught in words because it can't be explained by words.

I can't explain this to you, only tell you stories, so here are some stories showing other ways of seeing this so you can fully understand.

∞

∞

∞